Coconut

Constance L. Kirker is a retired Pennsylvania State University Professor of Art History, and an avid gardener and foodie.

Mary Newman has taught environmental health at Ohio University and the University of Malta.

Edible

Series Editor: Andrew F. Smith

Edible is a revolutionary series of books dedicated to food and drink that explores the rich history of cuisine. Each book reveals the global history and culture of one type of food or beverage.

Other Titles in the Series

Rice: A Global History by Renee Marton

Saffron: A Global History by Ramin Ganeshram

Chocolate: A Global History by Sarah Moss and Alexander Badenoch

Cocktails: A Global History by Joseph M. Carlin

Tea: A Global History by Helen Saberi

Coffee: A Global History by Jonathan Morris

Mango: A Global History by Constance L. Kirker and Mary Newman

Ice Cream: A Global History by Laura B. Weiss

Honey: A Global History by Lucy M. Long

Mustard: A Global History by Demet Güzey

Cheese: A Global History by Andrew Dalby

Cannabis: A Global History by Bradley J. Borougerdi

Forthcoming in the Series

Chillies: A Global History by Heather Arndt Anderson

Curry: A Global History by Colleen Taylor Sen

Spices: A Global History by Fred Czarra

Coconut

A Global History

CONSTANCE L. KIRKER
MARY NEWMAN

MACMILLAN

To our husbands, Tom and John, ever patient and encouraging on our coconutty adventure

First published in the United Kingdom 2022 by Reaktion Books Ltd
First published in India 2026 by Macmillan
an imprint of Pan Macmillan Publishing India Private Limited
707 Kailash Building
26 K. G. Marg, New Delhi 110001
www.panmacmillan.co.in

Pan Macmillan, The Smithson, 6 Briset St, Farringdon, London EC1M 5NR
Associated companies throughout the world
www.panmacmillan.com

ISBN 978-93-6113-990-1

1 3 5 7 9 8 6 4 2

Printed and bound in India by Thomson Press India Private Limited

MIX
Paper | Supporting responsible forestry
FSC® C010615

Contents

Introduction

The word 'coconut' conjures up visions of palm trees, cocktails and sunsets, instantly transporting us to a golden beach with blue skies and bluer water, a sweet cocktail in one hand and coconut-scented sunscreen slathered all over us. What could be more fun, engaging, interesting or seductive, even, than writing about the coconut?

The image of the coconut palm is often paired with other fascinating and strange images, from pagodas to pink flamingos, but always in a delightful way. Hawaiian, or 'aloha', shirts invariably feature coconut palms and are worn untucked, signalling a casual attitude of freedom in the wearer, declaring 'I am on holiday!' Former U.S. president Barack Obama, responding to a question about his future plans after he left office, said he could be found 'on a beach somewhere, drinking out of a coconut'.[1]

For those living in the Western world, which has a temperate climate in which coconut palms, by and large, simply cannot grow, the image, taste and, of course, smell of coconut are intriguing and extraordinary. Where coconut palms are abundant, they are much more than a sustaining food source. Where they are plentiful, people often remark that each household consumes at least one coconut daily and, in fact, a

President Obama drinking from a coconut in Luang Prabang, Laos, 2016.

common saying is, 'Without coconut there is no life.' Yet, for that very reason, the coconut seems to be taken for granted. People are surprised and dismayed to discover that the popularity of their beloved coconut water as a trendy superfood around the world has made its price skyrocket at home.

Consumers everywhere can easily identify the smell, texture and taste of coconut. Bags of processed, grated coconut are readily accessible at extremely reasonable prices, as are cans of coconut milk, cream or water. Recipes prepared with processed coconut, such as coconut layer cake or coconut cream pie, and the familiar coconut chocolate bar favourites Bounty, Mounds and Almond Joy are much-beloved treats in places where coconut palms do not grow.

Hopefully, some sections of this book will provide a trip down memory lane for readers who may recall favourite

Coconut palms in Kerala, India: the 'Land of Coconuts'.

coconut recipes from the 1950s and '60s, prepared with care and pride by mothers, grandmothers and aunts for special family occasions and church suppers. For example, the recipe for toasted coconut cream pie that has been enjoyed by the authors' family and friends for years turned out to be a 1950s recipe from the Tavern Restaurant in New York City. So treasured was this dessert that in 1958, Herb Hubschman, the owner of Two Guys department stores, called an aide in his office in Newark, New Jersey, and told her to send a Tavern coconut cream pie to him in Chicago, where he was attending a trade show. The aide bought a first-class aeroplane ticket for the pie and had it flown to Hubschman.

Many American readers may also have fond memories of ambrosia, not only named after the food or drink of the Greek gods but the go-to salad or dessert for many a potluck or shared dinner. Variations of this popular dish now feature pineapple, marshmallows, cherries or sour cream, augmenting

Mrs Watson's Toasted Coconut Cream Pie, adapted by the author's mother from a 1950s recipe created by New York's Tavern Restaurant.

the simple oranges and coconut of the first-known recipes recorded in cookbooks as early as the 1870s. Treats from cakes to puddings to hard sweets make up a large portion of the recipes that use coconut. This is not surprising, since sugar cane and coconut are both easily available and inexpensive in the tropical locations where they are grown, but there are many savoury applications as well.

Searching for coconut in the cuisines of countries in which it is grown and consumed fresh offers a different taste experience from sampling the processed, dried and preserved product more familiar in the West. Comparing freshly prepared coconut milk or grated coconut to even the finest brands of canned or packaged products is like the proverbial apples and oranges or chalk and cheese.

In places where the coconut grow freely, its extraordinary historical and cultural importance is acknowledged: for example, its use as prasad, or blessed food, in the Hindu tradition. Yet the culinary ingredient is so commonplace as to seem ordinary. Coconut is an essential element in many dishes of the spectacular feast known as a Sadya in Kerala, India. Coconut is so important in Sri Lanka that couples who are engaged would never consider having a wedding without it.

A cultural history of the coconut is not simply a matter of consulting traditional Western cultural sources such as the Bible, classical Greek and Roman texts, or Shakespeare and the Western literary canon for coconut references. Discovering the early history of the coconut and its importance requires searching out a more diverse range of references, such as Polynesian mythology and Indian Hindu traditions. Many food preparations have alternative names and spellings when translated into English.

Notable references to the coconut in the Western literary canon include Herman Melville, James A. Michener, Somerset

Maugham and Robert Louis Stevenson, who all used the South Pacific as a setting for their writing and made use of the coconut palm as an evocative icon. The plot of the novel *Mutiny on the Bounty*, by Charles Nordhoff and James Norman, hinges on a stolen coconut. Coconut appears in popular culture tropes such as the Pink Coconut Ice sweet for sale in Honeydukes wizarding sweet shop in J. K. Rowling's *Harry Potter and the Prisoner of Azkaban*.

Coconut has been aptly described as the 'Swiss Army knife of the plant kingdom'.[2] Unlike almost any other edible plant, there is virtually no part of the coconut tree or fruit that is not put to a useful purpose. In addition to being edible, parts of the coconut such as the shell, leaves and husks (coir) have broad utilitarian applications in cooking and growing food. Examples include being made into cooking and serving utensils, and even as the fuel used to cook food. Research today focuses on finding additional uses in every area of the world where coconut grows, from Sri Lanka and the Philippines, to Africa and the Caribbean. Governments, producers and entrepreneurs are all striving to capitalize on the current trend of high interest in all things coconut.

Some sources suggest that the pure water of a coconut was used as a life-sustaining substitute for blood plasma in emergency situations in the Pacific theatre of the Second World War. Though a theoretical possibility, there are no documented examples. What is certain is that in 1943, the adaptability and value of coconut was key to the curriculum of a survival course for American pilots during the Second World War in the Pacific. The goal was to prepare them for the possibility of being forced down and the necessity of using local flora and fauna, including the ubiquitous coconut, to sustain themselves. Americans from the U.S. mainland, most of whom would never have experienced coconut or other tropical plants, were instructed in the many ways coconut could be used for weaving clothing, providing containers and constructing emergency shelter, in addition to providing a source of food and fresh drinking water. Coconut husks can be used to ignite a ground oven and so, to conserve matches, could also light the soldiers' cigarettes.[3]

One of the most famous coconuts in the world sits on John F. Kennedy's desk in his presidential library in Boston, Massachusetts, as a reminder of how he and his crew were rescued on a Pacific island after their torpedo patrol boat was sunk in 1943 during the Second World War. Kennedy had carved a message noting their location on this coconut and passed it on to two Solomon Islanders who, at great risk to themselves, carried the message to Allied troops. After two days of surviving with only coconuts as nourishment, help arrived, and the inscribed coconut remained with Kennedy until his death.[4]

The coconut suggests metaphorical ways to understand the universe. Cook Island creation myths describe the cosmos as the hollow of a vast coconut shell, with the interior being the underworld and the outer shell being the upper world of mortals. The Malay use coconut as a device to express the meagre way in which humans understand their place on earth: 'A frog beneath a coconut shell believes there is no other world.' An expression from Zanzibar says, 'A coconut shell full of water is a sea to an ant.' An Indonesian expression employs the coconut to reflect an understanding of karma: 'The lot of the coconut shell is to float, and the lot of the stone is to sink.'

Charles Darwin understood the universe in a more scientific and practical way: researching what was to become his famous theory of evolution while sailing on HMS *Beagle* to the Cocos (Keeling) Islands in 1836, he mentioned coconut many times in his observations, describing coconut milk as pleasant and cool. He noted that native pigs on the island grew fat on a diet of coconut and made references to the coconut, or robber, crab and what was believed to be its aphrodisiac qualities.[5]

In 1912 Sir W. H. Lever, founder of Lever Brothers (one of the predecessors of consumer goods company Unilever), wrote of the coconut, 'I know of no field of tropical agriculture, that is so promising and I do not think in the whole world there is a promise of so lucrative an investment of time and money as in this industry.'[6] This remains true of the coconut palm today.

I

From Roots to Fruit: Botany, Production and Health

In 2016 authorities in the Indian state of Goa declassified the coconut palm as a tree, declaring it instead to be a grass. By this action, the coconut palm was no longer considered a protected tree, leaving thousands of palms vulnerable to destruction by property developers and industrial projects.

The coconut palm is much beloved by Goans, and the public outcry was swift and vociferous. Environmentalists hugged coconut palms and carried signs reading, 'Don't kill me, I'm a tree.' Social media buzzed in indignation. Surprised by the protests, the government of Goa rescinded the declassification of the coconut palm the following year, once again classifying it as a tree, and took the additional step of declaring the coconut palm the state tree of Goa.

Botanists have named the palm *Cocos nucifera*. The derivation of the word 'coconut' remains obscure, with some authorities believing its origin to be from the Spanish word *coco*, meaning 'grinning face'. Others think *cocos* is a Europeanized adaptation of the word *cocho*, used in the Philippines to describe the coconut.[1] *Nucifera* refers to the Latin term for 'nut-bearing'. An antiquated spelling for coconut is 'cocoanut', rarely used today as it leads to confusion with cocoa, which chocolate is made from.

There are over 1,500 species of palm trees in the world, but only one, *Cocos nucifera*, that produces coconuts.[2] Although there is only one species of coconut, there are many varieties, the two largest divisions being 'tall' and 'dwarf'. While tall palms are more robust and disease resistant, it takes eight to ten years for a newly planted tall palm to produce fruit. Dwarf palms can come into production in three years. The coconut water from a dwarf palm is sweeter and considered to be more flavourful. An important economic advantage of the dwarf palm is that it is shorter, making the harvesting of the coconuts considerably easier and more efficient. However, tall palms are more robust and disease-resistant.

Reproduction among coconut palm trees varies, depending upon whether the tree is of the tall or dwarf variety. In both, the flowers, called inflorescences, emerge from the frond. The male flower is situated at the tip of the branch, while the female flower is located further down. In tall varieties, the pollen is released from the male flower before the female flower of the same tree is ready to receive it, which means tall varieties must rely on cross-pollination for fertilization. The dwarf palms, however, are 90 per cent self-pollinating, as both the male and female flowers are simultaneously active.[3]

Most varieties are adaptations to diseases and environmental conditions (drought, as an example). Some variety names indicate the colour of the fruit. There is a mutant coconut that has an abnormal development of endosperm, resulting in the cavity being filled with a jelly-like flesh (called *kopyor* in Indonesia and *macapuno* in the Philippines) but virtually no water.

Regardless of the variety, the question remains: is the coconut a fruit or a nut? Botanically it is neither, but it does have qualities of both in its culinary uses at various stages of

Parts of a coconut, from Herman Adolph Köhler's *Medizinal-Pflanzen* (1887).

its development; this may have led to the confusion. A young coconut has a jelly-like texture and is often called a fruit. The hard, white coconut meat that is grated is more like a nut. The coconut is technically termed 'a fibrous drupe', a stone fruit in which an outer fleshy part surrounds a single shell of hardened endocarp, with a kernel inside.

Coconuts have a smooth outside skin called the exocarp, which varies in colour, ranging from green to red or brown. The mesocarp is the fibrous husk beneath it. The shell is the endocarp that encloses the kernel called the endosperm. The testa is the thin, brown coat on the endosperm. The endosperm is the white flesh and may be about 12 millimetres (½ in.) thick. The cavity contains water, the volume of which decreases with maturity.

The maximum age of a coconut palm is one hundred to two hundred years. In its most productive years, between fifteen and thirty, a tall coconut annually produces one hundred nuts.[4] A dwarf palm produces approximately 20 per cent less than tall palms per tree, but dwarf palms can be planted in higher density, producing the same yield per unit of area.

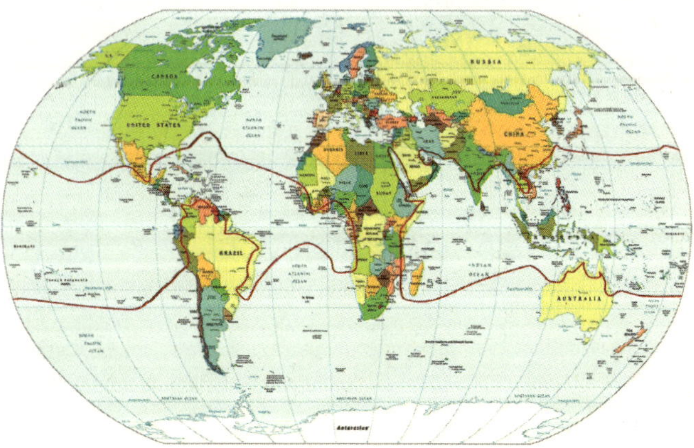

World map of coconut-growing regions.

Coconut palms grow between 23° north and 23° south of the equator. If the tree survives outside this limit, it doesn't produce fruit. Coconut palms flourish in sandy soil that is aerated and well drained. They do best in temperatures between 27°C (81°F) and 30°C (86°F), and although they tolerate salt water, they do require fresh groundwater and humid environments.[5]

Indonesia is the world's largest producer of coconuts, with the Philippines coming in a close second.[6] India is number three in production. These three countries account for about 70 per cent of the world's total production of coconuts. Brazil, Sri Lanka and Vietnam follow as fourth, fifth and sixth, respectively.[7] More than 10 million smallholder and sharecropper families with farms of less than 4 hectares (10 ac) grow about 96 per cent of the worldwide coconut crop. About 70 per cent of the total production is consumed domestically.[8]

About 17 billion coconuts are harvested worldwide, which translates to more than 80 million people earning their livelihoods through the growing and processing of coconut.[9] Of the just under 110 million people in the Philippines, there are 1.5 million coconut farmers, and more than 24 million other people involved in coconut growing or processing.[10]

Coconut oil is an important export commodity, with the Philippines exporting over 1 million tonnes. Indonesia exports 500,000 tonnes. The largest importers are Europe, with more than 700,000 tonnes, with the United States second, at 600,000 tons.[11] The Netherlands serves as the main port for importation of these coconut products into Europe, which are then distributed to other countries. Coconut oil is particularly popular in France and Germany.[12]

It is not only human workers who are trained to harvest coconuts, a dangerous high-wire task. Many consumers of

Boys in the Philippines drinking fresh coconut.

Thai coconuts would be surprised to learn that their coconuts had been harvested by pig-tailed macaques. Arjen Schoevers, an instructor at a Thai monkey training school, notes, 'It would be difficult to find a coconut product made in Thailand that wasn't picked by a monkey.'[13] The rationale for using monkeys as harvesters is based primarily on economics. A trained male macaque can pick 1,600 coconuts a day, while a female can pick six hundred. Comparing that to the human production of eighty coconuts per day, even eliminating costs for workers' pay and benefits, it is easy to appreciate why monkeys are used. Accounts and illustrations show that monkeys have been used to harvest coconuts going back as far as 2500 BCE.[14] Monkey labour is controversial, of course, with animal-rights activists equating it to slave labour, but the practice persists, even after a 2009 report from Thailand of one rebellious macaque named Brother Kwan heaving a coconut at his owner's head, killing him.

In 1902 one wide-eyed visionary believed the coconut was beneficial to one's health and a panacea for mankind's ills, as well as a path to oneness with God. August Engelhardt was a sun-worshipping German nudist and a radical 'cocovore'. From 1902 to 1919 he lived on the island of Kabakon in what is now Papua New Guinea, subsisting entirely on coconuts. He believed that, because coconuts grew high up on the tree, closest to the sun and, to his mind, closest to God, the coconut was godlike. And because the coconut resembled the human head, Engelhardt believed being a cocovore also made one a theophage, an 'eater of God'.

At least fifteen young persons voyaged to Engelhardt's island, where they joined his *Sonnenorden* (Order of the Sun) cult. Things did not go well. Several of them died, and the others returned to Germany, sick and furious with Engelhardt.

The recluse continued to live in his less-than-idyllic island paradise and died at the age of 44, rheumatic, ulcerated, mentally ill and reduced to a bag of bones.[15]

Although at one point he had 4,000 followers in Ben Tre Province, Vietnam, in the 1960s, the Coconut Monk, Nguyen Thanh Nam, was equally unsuccessful in establishing the Coconut religion, which advocated consuming only coconuts and drinking only coconut milk.[16]

Neera is the sap collected from the unopened coconut flowers, the inflorescences, and is enclosed in a sheath called the spathe. When the spathe is cut, sap flows. A tree can produce 300–400 litres (80–105 gallons) of sap per year. Sap is collected in the morning by tree-climbing 'toddy tappers'. If the collected sap is boiled, coconut sugar is produced as liquid syrup, a solid block or granules. If the sap is allowed to ferment, an alcoholic drink called *toddy* in India and *tuba* in the Philippines is formed. Toddy can also be used as a leavening agent similar to yeast. Aged sap can be used to make coconut aminos, a gluten-free, soy-free substitute for soy sauce. Vinegar can be made from either coconut sap or coconut water. Coconut vinegar is used to make *acar* (raw vegetable pickles) in Indonesia, Malaysia and Singapore, and may be a replacement for apple cider vinegar, or a fad weight-loss supplement. Coconut wine in the Philippines is known as *lambanog*, and a coconut wine festival, Sanggutan, is held there in May.

Coconut flowers are edible. In indigenous populations, the flowers are mixed with curdled milk and fed to people suffering from diabetes. A more interesting use of coconut flowers is when they are presented to newly-weds as an aphrodisiac.[17]

Coconut water has been part of traditional medicine since ancient times. The water has antioxidant properties and has

Making coconut sugar by boiling neera, Java, Indonesia.

been used for liver, kidney, gastric and reproductive disorders.[18] First introduced into the United States in 2004, coconut water quickly became a strong competitor to commercial sports drinks because of its impressive electrolyte content. The water of young coconuts (called 'tender' coconuts) is preferred because it has a more pleasing taste than that of more mature coconuts.

Coconut flowers. Flowering occurs continuously and female flowers are pollinated by insects and wind.

The coconut kernel is the solid endosperm of the fruit. It has a thin brown layer, called the testa, which is usually peeled off to expose the white coconut kernel. The testa peelings are usually discarded or used for animal feed, but can also be used for smoking meats.

Coconut milk is made by adding water to the kernel and squeezing it through a press or strainer. It is usually purchased in cans in areas where coconut trees do not grow. Sometimes the coconut milk is sprayed and dried to make coconut milk powder as another way of preserving it. The milk makes a great base for smoothies, soups and curries. In some recipes, as in Omani chicken coconut curry, the coconut powder is pan-roasted to add a unique toasted flavour.

Coconut oil is another important product that comes from the kernel and has both industrial and culinary applications. Coconut oil used in industry as a lubricant is derived from the copra, the dried kernel. In culinary usage, however, virgin coconut oil is pressed from fresh coconut kernels without heat or chemicals applied. If the coconut trees are grown without chemical pesticides, the oil can then be labelled as organic virgin coconut oil, commanding a higher market price. Coconut oil stands up to heat and can be used for frying. But using coconut oil as a cooking oil has been controversial. The issue of whether the fats in coconut are healthy is illustrated in these two article headlines: 'Coconut Oil Isn't Healthy. It's Never Been Healthy', and 'Yes, Coconut Oil Is Still Healthy. It's Always Been Healthy'.[19]

Making coconut milk by hand in Kerala, India.

For a number of years, medical professionals have expressed warnings about the possible dangerous health effects of saturated fats – as opposed to unsaturated fats – in our cooking oils and foods. The saturated fats in coconut have not escaped the saturated versus unsaturated debate. But the saturated fats in coconut oil are medium-chain triglycerides, which may have some health benefits, rather than the long-chain triglycerides associated with heart disease. Between 46 and 54 per cent of the fat in coconut oil is lauric acid.[20] Lauric acid is a relatively rare saturated fatty acid in nature, the two main sources of lauric acid in the human diet being coconut milk and human breast milk. Some researchers believe that the fats in coconut oil are not as harmful as other types of saturated fats. Others suggest that coconut oil may help to lower the risks of heart attack and stroke, while the American Heart Association has stated that there are no known 'off-setting favorable effects' in using coconut oil. The debate rages on.[21]

The coconut meat has many uses. Grated and desiccated, it can be preserved for long periods of time. It can be sweetened and used in making confectionery and desserts, or left unsweetened for use in savoury dishes.

Coconut meat, after it has been pressed for virgin coconut oil, can also be dried and ground to form a flour. The flour is very high in fibre and protein, low in carbohydrates and gluten free. The commercial food industry uses coconut flour to increase fibre content in various products such as energy bars. So that nothing is wasted, residue from coconut processing for industrial oils can be fed to animals such as pigs. It is said that the pork produced from pigs that are fed this diet is particularly tasty.

The roots of the coconut tree serve as a coffee substitute. Indigenous healers have used the root as a diuretic to treat

Using mechanical means to complete the tough task of grating coconut, Cebu, the Philippines.

urinary disorders, and it has been considered effective for reducing fevers.[22]

Coconut leaves are used to wrap food for steaming, which imparts a delicate coconut flavour to the food. Rice steamed in packets woven with coconut leaves is called *puto* in the Philippines and *ketaput* in Indonesia. These packets are sold on the street and in restaurants to accompany curries. Some dishes are cooked over burning coconut husks, giving them a smoky flavour. *Bibingka* is a sweet Filipino rice flour and coconut dish baked over burning coconut husks. This dish is traditionally served in the Philippines at Christmastime but is also a common street food served with *puto*.

Cooking bibinka with coconut husks, the Philippines.

When terminal buds of the coconut tree are used in a salad, it is called 'millionaire's salad', because an entire tree is sacrificed when the buds are cut from it. When boiled, the bud tastes like cabbage.

Coconut shells may be fashioned into cups, ladles, bowls and cooking vessels for some foods. Shells cut in half make percussive musical instruments for the Filipino coconut dance and famously provided the sound of horses' hooves in the film *Monty Python and the Holy Grail* (1975). The trunk of the coconut palm may also be fashioned into a variety of utensils and serving items, as it is an attractive wood known as porcupine wood.

Coconuts may be eaten in various stages of their maturity. Thais particularly like the taste of very young coconut meat, which has an almost jelly-like consistency; young coconuts are sometimes called 'Thai coconuts'. A classic example of the use of young coconut meat in Thai cuisine is coconut soup, which is made from strips of young coconut meat. Young coconut is cut into strips and used as noodles in some Thai savoury dishes. The Filipino *buko* pie is made from young coconuts.

Coconut sprout displayed by a coconut grower, Kerala, India.

The type of coconut we are most familiar with in the West is the mature coconut. These are the tan- to brown-coloured 'hairy' coconuts with three 'eyes' resembling a human face. It is a challenge for anyone inexperienced in breaking them open to do so and extract the meat.

A past ripe or fully mature coconut may start to sprout inside and produce an edible 'fluff'. Botanically, it is called the haustorium, sometimes coconut sprout, coconut apple, coconut cotyledon or coconut embryo. It is eaten raw and has a crunchy yet spongy, watery, sweet taste somewhat similar to an apple. It is known as *iho* or *lolo* in Hawaii, where, in the past, only the royals were allowed to eat it. *Iho* was considered powerful because it contained the life force of a new tree and so was reserved only for those in power.

All around the world, people are enjoying the culinary delights offered by coconut. But where did it all begin?

2
A Long and Fabled Story

The brothers thought that it was a great idea to steal the canoe they found on the beach and use it for fishing. Had they known that the Devil owned the canoe, they certainly would never have stolen it. But now, with the canoe filled with fish, the Devil was in hot pursuit.

The brothers paddled madly, but the devil, an excellent swimmer, was gaining on them. One brother scooped up armfuls of fish, flinging them overboard. The Devil swallowed them all and kept coming.

Terrified and desperate, a hideous idea came to the brothers' minds simultaneously. Grabbing their knives, the brothers set upon each other in a last-ditch struggle. The younger brother emerged victorious, cut his brother's corpse into pieces – all except the head – and flung them into the Devil's gaping maw.

This surprise delicacy stopped the Devil in his tracks, and the younger brother escaped to shore, where he buried his brother's head. From that head sprang the first coconut tree, or at least that was how the origin of the coconut was explained to many generations in the Admiralty Islands.[1]

There are numerous other coconut creation stories worldwide, often involving both violence and the burying of a

Coconut trade card, early 1900s.

head, tales no doubt influenced by how much the coconut resembles the human head, with its two eyes and a nose.

Looking to palaeobotany to help answer the riddle of the origin of the coconut, fossils dating from the Miocene Age (*c.* 23 million to 5 million years ago) that are similar to today's coconut have been found in New Zealand. In west-central India, coconut fossils have been found that are believed to be even older, from the Early Eocene Age, 30 to 50 million years ago.[2]

Researchers have examined the DNA of more than 1,300 specimens of coconut trees throughout the world and have determined that the coconut was first brought under cultivation in two separate locations, in the Pacific Ocean basin and in the Indian Ocean basin. B. F. Gunn, in 'Independent Origins of Cultivated Coconut (*Cocos nucifera* L.) in the Old World Tropics' (2011), wrote,

> The impact of the coconut palm (*Cocos nucifera* L.) on the history of human dispersal in the humid tropics is unparalleled in the plant kingdom. The history of dispersal and cultivation of this species is thus fundamentally intertwined with human history in the tropics.[3]

According to N. M. Nayer in *The Coconut: Phylogeny, Origins, and Spread* (2017), the French botanists Emile Massal and Jacques Barrau observed, 'human life on the atolls would scarcely be possible without coconuts.'[4]

There is controversy about whether coconuts spread through natural dispersal by floating to a new location, or solely through human intervention. The argument for natural dispersal is based on the buoyancy and salt tolerance of the coconut, provided by its thick husk and the cavity within the shell.[5] Studies have shown that a coconut may float for up to four months and can successfully take root if it reaches a shore where the necessary space and nutrients are available. Still a hazard, however, are local fauna such as the coconut crab, described by Charles Darwin on his famous voyage to the Cocos Islands in 1836 as 'monstrous'. The largest terrestrial arthropod in the world, with a leg span of up to 1 metre (3 ft), a coconut crab has the strength to break open coconuts and will feast on this delight before the coconut has a chance to sprout.

But there is no doubt that coconuts were also dispersed through human intervention, especially by migrating Polynesians. Imagine packing to leave the only home you have ever known, for a journey of unknown length, to an unknown place – you would definitely include your favourite and most reliable foods. Food historian Rachel Laudan describes the prehistoric culinary package that people on the oceanic side of New Guinea, possibly around 1000 BCE, would likely have assembled to feed themselves on their dangerous voyage exploring islands of the Pacific.[6] An important item would have been the coconut, which provided both the necessary convenient and safe drinking water and was also a source of food.

Polynesia was populated by these migrant seafarers travelling eastbound from Indonesia. They settled on islands where they found conditions favourable for growing coconuts and tropical plants. Eventually, they brought coconuts to Hawaii, near the northern boundary of today's coconut-growing region. Through natural drift and human activity, including trade and migration, areas for successfully propagating coconuts were established in parts of India and Southwest Asia. Culinary historians have determined that as early as 1500 BCE, coconut was a common element in the diet of the Harappan civilization on the Indian subcontinent.

In the sixth century, Arab merchants controlled the trade routes, bringing spices and coconuts to East Africa and ports along the Red Sea. Caravans would then distribute these products. In the 'Tale of Sinbad the Sailor', a story from the *Arabian Nights Entertainment* or *One Thousand and*

One Nights, Sinbad buys and sells coconuts during his fifth voyage:

> Then, going to the captain of the ship, I agreed with him for my passage and embarked my coconuts and what else I possessed. We weighed anchor the same day and sailed from island to island and sea to sea, and whenever we stopped, I sold and traded with my coconuts, and the Lord requited me more than I erst had and lost.[7]

In the thirteenth century, the Italian explorer Marco Polo enlightened Europe about the coconut, which he referred to as *Nux indica* in the book of his voyage to Asia, *The Travels of Marco Polo*. He dubbed it the 'Pharaoh's Nut' after encountering coconuts in India. Describing the nut, he writes,

> This description of the coco-nut (*Cocos nucifera*) is well known, even to those who have only seen the fruits as brought to Europe, to be perfectly just; but the grateful refreshment afforded by its liquor when drunk from the young nut, whilst the outer husk is green and the kernel still gelatinous, can only be judged of by those who have travelled, under a fervid sun, in those countries where it is produced.[8]

A coconut origin story from India is related by Ibn Battuta, writing in the 1300s. The coconut, especially that of the islands of Dhibat al-Mahal (the Maldives), is the size of a human head, and the island's residents tell this story:

> A certain philosopher in India in past ages was in the service of one of the kings and was held by him in high esteem. The king had a vizier, between whom and this

philosopher there was enmity. The philosopher said to the king, 'if this vizier's head is cut off and buried, there will bring advantage to the people of India and other peoples in the world.' The king said to him, 'And what if this that you have stated does not come from the head of the vizier?' He replied, 'if it does not, do with my head as you have done with his.' So the king gave orders to cut off the vizier's head, and the philosopher took it, planted a date-seed in his head, and tended it until it grew into a tree and produced this nut as its fruit.[9]

Portuguese explorers discovered a sea route to the riches of India by sailing around the Cape of Good Hope. After Vasco da Gama brought coconuts from India to Europe in 1498, the Portuguese established outposts in India and developed a lucrative trade in products from the Indian subcontinent. The Portuguese were soon followed by the Spanish, Dutch and British, all vying to control the spice trade. In 1501 King Manuel of Portugal wrote a letter to Ferdinand and Isabella of Spain, 'extolling the prime value of coconuts as a source of drinking water and cordage for sailing ships'.[10]

During the sixteenth century, the Portuguese established coconut plantations in their colonies on the West and East African coasts, the Cabo Verde archipelago, the Caribbean and Brazil. By the 1670s the Spanish had also planted coconut palms in their New World colonies, including Mexico. Spanish coconut plantations in Colima, Mexico, were producing 'marvelous' wine, likely making use of technology developed in their colonies in the Philippines.[11]

Years later, coconut was an important part of the food supply for the 1769 scientific voyage of Captain James Cook. His men traded with the indigenous people for coconut at

Detail of a Portuguese merchant with coconut and scale, from a 15th-century edition of Dioscorides' *Tractatus de herbis*. The merchant's scales allude to the coconut's value in Europe.

what may seem exorbitant exchange rates. For example, they traded ten coconuts for a white glass bead.[12]

In 1789 Captain William Bligh punished the entire crew of HMS *Bounty* by cutting their rum ration in half, in retribution for the theft of a single coconut from the captain's private larder. A coconut cup once belonging to the captain, inscribed with the words, 'The cup I eat my miserable allowance of', was auctioned at Christie's of London in 2002 for £71,700 ($110,000).[13]

Hans van Amsterdam, mounted coconut cup, 1535, silver gilt and coconut shell.

Records in museum collections reveal that Arab traders carried coconut shells overland to Europe as early as the first century; there they were treated as rare, valuable objects, fashioned into ritual cups and even decorated with precious metals. These goblets became prized possessions of popes and kings dating back to at least 1200 and were especially popular in Great Britain and Northern Europe.[14] By the eighteenth century, coconuts had lost their rarity and were more accessible to ordinary citizens in the American colonies, who would likely possess a simple functional coconut ladle.

Coconuts were just one of many products brought to worldwide attention through European colonial exploitation. The chequered history of colonialism is apparent in this coconut origin story from Indonesia: in a dream, a man named Ameta is instructed to plant the mysterious object he had discovered while hunting boar. After planting it, a magnificent palm tree sprouts and blossoms. Nine days later, Ameta finds that the blossom has transformed into a little girl, whom he adopts and names Hainuwele, which means 'coconut branch'. Hainuwele gains maturity and discovers she has an amazing skill – she is able to defecate valuable items such as 'golden earrings, coral, porcelain dishes, bush-knives, copper boxes, and gongs'.[15] Her father, Ameta, becomes a rich man. As Hainuwele excretes increasingly valuable gifts for Ameta, jealousy and greed consume the villagers. Deciding her powers are unnatural, they kill her by burying her alive.

The tale, from the Maluku Islands, was first recorded in the 1930s by the German ethnologist Adolf E. Jensen. An interesting interpretation of the story points out the evils of colonialism. Coconut production, symbolized by Hainuwele, the Coconut Girl, may bring wealth, symbolized by the trade goods she excretes to the islanders. In this explanation of the meaning of the story, the tale represents the rise of greed and inequality in the society, resulting from a material-based culture imported by foreigners and colonial oppressors. Other less political interpretations consider the story to be about the origins of agriculture and the crops from the earth, including tubers that Hainuwele introduces.[16]

Before coconuts were established internationally as a food product, they were a valuable commercial asset, with different parts of the coconut used for a variety of purposes. Trading ships used coconuts as dunnage and a supply of fresh water. Coir, or the 'hair' of the coconut, was woven into strong, waterproof ropes and mats, and copra, the dried 'meat' of the coconut, was used in making industrial oil, soap and candles.

Beginning in the mid-nineteenth century, the major European colonial powers began coconut cultivation in their various spheres of influence, from India to Sri Lanka, Africa, the East Indies and the Pacific region. Large-scale planting of coconuts for commercial export of oil and dried copra began in South Pacific regions. Commercial coconut plantations were established by European entrepreneurs who recognized that the indigenous populations could be a source of cheap labour. By 1892 the Portuguese had developed one of the largest company-owned coconut plantations in the world in their East African colony of Mozambique.

In 1887 F. W. Loder invented a process for refining coconut oil that would make it more palatable and, therefore, a suitable substitute for oleo oil and margarine. After the Spanish–American War, when Spain ceded the Philippines to the United States, coconut exports to the United States rose. Not only was coconut oil used in margarine, but copra was used to create industrial oil.

Another culinary use for coconut oil developed in England in the late nineteenth century, when large soap

Vicente Albán, *Lady with Black Slave and Coconut*, 1783, oil on canvas.

manufacturers using coconut oil put the smaller manufacturers out of business. These smaller businesses retooled their machinery and, still using coconut oil, started deep-frying fish and chips.[17] Fish and chip establishments today are advised that, while less affordable than vegetable oils, coconut oil is the healthiest option for deep-frying fish.[18]

In the 1800s Alfred Nobel discovered that glycerine, a by-product of manufacturing soap, could be used in making explosives, and for some years, coconut soap manufacturing became a very profitable business until synthetic substitutes for nitroglycerine were developed.[19]

By the turn of the century, advances in technology, such as machinery that produces desiccated coconut, created new opportunities for exporting coconut for culinary use. Operating in Sri Lanka (then known as Ceylon), the British entrepreneur Henry Vavasseur developed a process for grating and then drying coconut meat. This dried product could

A water-buffalo-driven train ambles through a Franklin Baker plantation in the Philippines after harvesting coconuts, 1950s.

be shipped more easily than whole coconuts and would not spoil in transit.[20]

A major player in the production and marketing of desiccated coconut is the Franklin Baker Company. Its story began in 1894 in Philadelphia, when flour merchant Franklin

Baker received a boatload of fresh coconuts as payment from a Cuban merchant for flour that Baker had shipped to Cuba. Baker developed a method to shred and produce coconut meat of uniform quality and was instrumental in promoting the use of shredded coconut to local housewives as a food product. The company continues to be a global leader in producing desiccated coconut from its facilities in the Philippines.[21]

During the Second World War, the availability of coconut sharply declined because of the conflict in the South Pacific region. Americans discovered that soybean oil could replace coconut oil, and once the war had ended, a strong soybean lobby was able to effectively keep the re-emerging supply of coconut oil out of the manufacturing of margarine.

Coconut has also found its way into the world of intoxicating libations. Originating in California in the 1930s, Tiki culture is defined by motifs idealizing tropical regions of the South Pacific. The exotically decorated bars and restaurants feature alcoholic cocktails made with a coconut milk base and coconut cream. Tiki culture grew more popular with the return of U.S. servicemen from the Pacific after the Second World War and continues to be a retro theme for parties today.

In 1952 Puerto Ricans developed cream of coconut and invented the pina colada, which has been their national drink since 1978. It has since gained worldwide attention through the development of luxury hotels on the island. But coconut in its alcoholic form was not welcomed everywhere. In India in the 1940s, Mahatma Gandhi spoke out against the social decline he partly attributed to toddy, an alcoholic drink made from neera, coconut sap. The Indian state of Tamil Nadu outlawed the making and selling of toddy in 1948, but that law was overturned 23 years later. Consumption of alcohol, including toddy, is prohibited in the states of Bihar, Gujarat and Nagaland and in all of India on days of festivals and national holidays, or 'Dry Days'.

Historically, coconut has been a major ingredient with an identifiable flavour in South Asian and Southeast Asian cuisines and is used in both savoury and sweet dishes. The creative culinary uses of coconut and coconut products continue to expand globally. An interesting example of this expansion is the way coconut has been effectively used in Thai-government-sponsored 'culinary diplomacy'. In an effort to promote Thai culture internationally, in 2001 the Thai government instituted a programme through which it would help entrepreneurs from Thailand to open Thai restaurants abroad by providing funding, training, supplies and even appropriate decorations. With a goal of establishing Thai restaurants internationally and

Workers removing the outer skin of coconuts for processing, Franklin Baker Company, San Pablo City, the Philippines.

promoting the nation's cuisine, the Global Thai Restaurant Company Ltd was widely successful. Approximately 15,000 restaurants were opened under the programme, including more than 5,000 in the United States, a country where the population of immigrants from Thailand and Americans of Thai descent is only about 300,000. In preparation for this programme, the Thai government conducted focus group research with American consumers. They found that coconut dishes, such as *kaeng phet* (red curry), *kaeng khiao wan* (green curry), *tom kha gai* (Thai chicken coconut soup) and *khao neeo mamuang* (mango with sticky rice), were very popular and have since become iconic examples of Thai cuisine enjoyed worldwide.[22] Food manufacturers are experimenting with coconut-flavoured M&Ms and red-curry-flavoured crisps, among other innovative products to add to the long culinary history of the coconut.

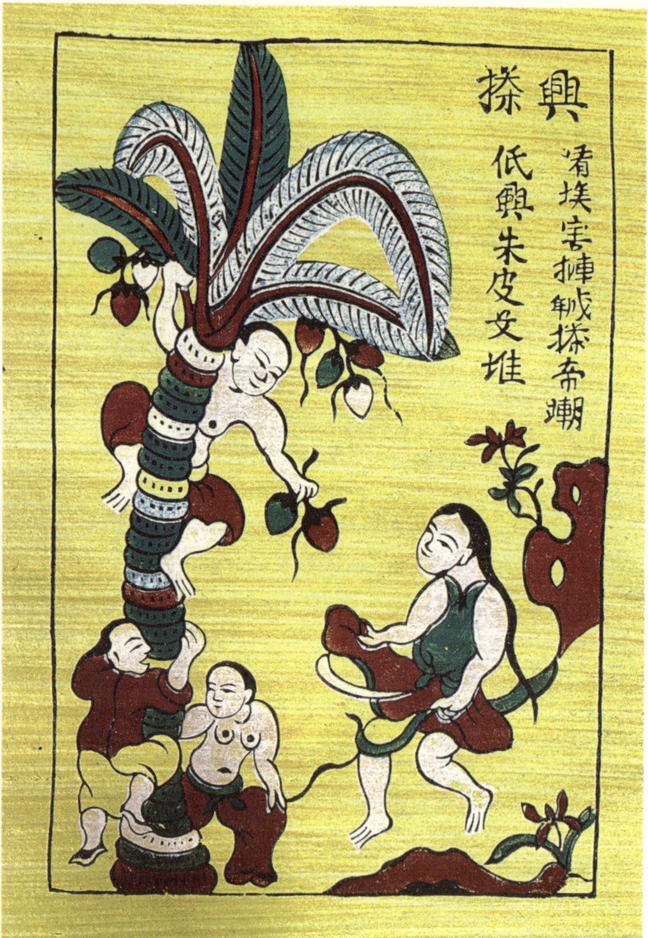

Contemporary Vietnamese Dong Ho woodblock print showing the coconut harvest.

3

Southeast Asia and China

Geographic neighbours Vietnam, Thailand, Cambodia, Myanmar, Malaysia and Laos share the liberal use of coconut in their cuisines. While each has developed some of its own unique dishes, many food preparations have similar ingredients and techniques with different local names.

Coconut is a staple in Vietnamese cooking, used in both savoury and sweet dishes. While coconut water is used for braising, larger pieces of grated coconut are used as toppings, and coconut milk is essential to many savoury curries. Sticky rice is often cooked with coconut milk. Many species of Vietnamese fish and even frog legs are stir-fried with coconut milk.

At the U.S. Embassy in Hanoi in 2017, the partner of the U.S. Ambassador to Vietnam described his delight in sharing the experience of learning to make traditional sweets for Tet, the Vietnamese lunar new year. Sweets play an important role in the celebrations, representing a wish for sweet new beginnings, and are liberally shared with family and friends. White and multicoloured coconut ribbons, *mut dura*, are an essential element of the *mam ngu qua*, or 'five-fruit tray', which is offered to guests. If a family is not making their own home-made sweets, they are likely to purchase them from traditional confectioners in Ben Tre province, who distribute coconut sweets throughout the country and abroad.

Banh phu the, 'husband and wife' cakes, or 'marriage' cakes, are made for Vietnamese wedding banquets using mung bean paste filling and a variety of other ingredients from various parts of the country, including coconut flakes and coconut milk. They are traditionally wrapped in a perfectly folded origami-like square box created from coconut leaves. The sticky texture is meant to remind the couple of the stickiness of their marriage ties. The filling is thought to symbolize the

Authors help make Vietnamese coconut 'marriage' cakes for a family wedding, 2017.

'embrace and protection of spousal love'.[1] Additional meaning is sometimes ascribed to each of the five colours of the cakes, representing the Chinese philosophy of the five elements (wood, fire, earth, metal and water). Vietnamese cuisine is highly influenced by Chinese medicine and philosophy. The coconut meat and the flour are white (metal), the mung bean filling is yellow (earth), sesame seeds are black (water), coconut leaves are green (wood), and the tiny square package would be wrapped in a red tie (fire).

Banh bo hap, pastel-coloured, sweet, spongy steamed rice cakes made from rice flour, water, sugar, yeast and coconut milk, are another popular Tet treat, and are known by several different names. Literally translated, *banh* means 'cake', but *bo* can mean 'cow' – as the cakes resemble a cow's udder – or 'crawl', referring to the way the cakes crawl or puff up when steamed.

Both coconuts and mung beans are known for their cooling properties and are important ingredients in *che dau xanh*, coconut milk-based dessert soups. Variously containing lotus seeds, colourful fruits and lots of ice, these treats are especially popular in the summer months. Coconut cream is often used as a garnish before serving.

Unique to Vietnamese cuisine is a delicacy of the Mekong River Delta area known as *duong dua*: coconut worm larvae (*Rhynchophorus ferrugineus*). The dish is thought to enhance male sexuality and is very expensive, selling for as much as U.S.$1 per worm. The *duong dua* beetle embeds itself in a healthy coconut, piercing one of the holes and laying the eggs in it. Once the eggs hatch, the larvae grow by eating the coconut tree shoots, essentially destroying the tree. In fact, the species is designated as invasive and harmful, and it is illegal to breed it. Banned by the Vietnamese Plant Protection Department since 2001, the dish is even more enticing to some. Aficionados are said to eat the coconut-fattened larvae alive, dipped in a chilli fish sauce.[2]

There is a tradition of wearing protective amulets in Thai Buddhism, and a coconut with one hole or eye, a rare mutation in the fruit, is considered to be particularly auspicious. Small amulets made from these special coconuts can sell for hundreds of dollars.

Some Thai foods are considered good luck and offer powers of protection. Of the 'Nine Auspicious Desserts', described as a Thai culinary treasure, coconut is an ingredient in four. Each of the beautifully presented sweets has a particular meaning. Originally prepared with complicated methods only for the Thai king or royal family, royal Thai cuisine recipes dating from the period of the Ayutthaya Kingdom (1351–1767) were once closely guarded secrets. These stunningly beautiful dishes are now enjoyed by all on very special occasions, including weddings and Buddhist celebrations.

Khanom chan is a Thai layer jelly cake with nine colourful stacked layers, or *chan*, that symbolize advancement in career and continual success. *Med kanoon* (Thai green peanut paste) is a sweet that symbolizes the support provided by friends and family for the success of a wedding couple – the word *noon* in Thai means 'support'. This treat is made from mashed, steamed mung bean with coconut milk which, when thickened, is shaped into a ball, dipped into egg yolk and cooked in syrup.

Ja mong gut refers to the traditional reverence for a king – *mongkut* means 'crown' in Thai. In the past, this dessert was prepared only for the Thai royal family. Even today, *ja mong gut* is rarely found in the market or bakeries because of its complicated production and the difficult elaborate carving required. The process of making *ja mong gut* can take up to seven hours.

Served in celebration of an important job promotion, the dessert has a shape similar to a crown and represents an important and respected professional position, as well as the hope for future success.

The sweet *sanay chan* represents the love life of the bride and groom, hopefully as beautiful as a full moon shining brightly in the night sky. Its ingredients are ground coconut mixed with flour, sugar, egg yolk, rice flour and a light touch of nutmeg.

'Coconut is Life' is the theme of one of the most important coconut festivals in Southeast Asia, held in the Thai city of Koh Phangan to celebrate all the possibilities of coconut. Coconut-based sweets are an important part of the water festival Songkran, a New Year celebration shared by Buddhists

Thai mango and sticky rice dessert.

in Thailand, Myanmar, Cambodia and Laos. In Myanmar, sweet snacks are known collectively as *moun*. Especially popular during the Buddhist New Year water festivals, most sweets are coconut based.

An argument might be made that it is through exposure to Thai cuisine that many Westerners are first introduced to coconut as a savoury ingredient in addition to its many uses in sweet desserts. Thai cuisine is known for its balance of four fundamental flavours in each dish, or in the overall meal – spicy, sour, sweet and salty. Along with the ubiquitous Thai dessert *khao niaow ma muang*, mango with sticky rice and coconut sauce, virtually every menu in any Thai restaurant will include the savoury coconut dishes *tom kha gai* (chicken coconut soup), *kaeng phet* (Thai red curry) and *kaeng khiao*

Thai *massaman* curry, Kalaya restaurant, Philadelphia.

(Thai green chicken curry), among others. Thai *massaman* curry, always made with coconut milk, was voted the number one dish in a CNN survey of the world's most delicious foods in 2011.

A recent goal of the Thai government is to make Thailand a major world food exporter, emphasizing quality standards and technology, under the ambitious slogan of 'Thailand: Kitchen of the World'. Thai coconuts are exported worldwide and even high-end food shops on the island of Hainan, China, where coconuts grow virtually everywhere, import beautifully prepared and plastic-wrapped fresh coconuts from Thailand. There are Thai food sections in larger supermarkets, and speciality items such as coconut-flavoured M&Ms and red-curry-flavoured crisps appear on grocery shelves beyond the ethnic or world food aisles.

According to the *Financial Times*, the recent appearance of authentic Thai food in British pubs is somewhat surprising and the product of a happy accident.[3] In 1988 Gerry O'Brien, the Irish manager of the Churchill Arms in Notting Hill Gate, London, hired Thai chef Khoyachai Sampaothong on a trial basis to upgrade his evening food offerings. More than thirty years later, there are numerous Thai restaurants located in traditional British pubs throughout London, virtually all serving various traditional Thai curries and soups featuring coconut.

Westerners have considerably less exposure to Cambodian food. Similar to a Thai preparation, Cambodian *amok* is widely considered to be the national dish of Cambodia. The word *amok* refers to the process of steaming curry in banana leaves. Thick coconut cream, as well as galangal, similar to ginger, are both essential ingredients.

A coconut pancake called *khao nom kok* is a favourite street food in Laos, and is also available in Thailand, Myanmar and

Lao coconut pancakes, *khao nom kok*.

Indonesia. These 7.5-centimetre (3 in.) half-moon-shaped coconut pancakes are prepared on a special griddle, with sweet and savoury toppings available. According to a sad Lao legend, a boy and girl fall in love against the wishes of the girl's father. The father constructs a trap to capture and kill the unfortunate young man, but as the daughter tries to rescue her lover from the trap, both of them are killed. *Khao nom kok* are to be eaten on the anniversary of this sad event each year, the sixth day of the waning moon of the sixth lunar month, which roughly corresponds to a day in the second half of July.

Laotian *nam vahn* is a coconut-milk-based dessert, which includes tapioca and local tropical fruits – jackfruits, lychees and longans. *Mee kati* is a sweet rice vermicelli soup made in coconut milk. *Khao lam* is a sweet, sticky rice dish made with red beans, coconut, coconut milk and sugar prepared in bamboo. Similar to *cendol* in Malaysia, *lod xong* is a dessert featuring green, worm-like noodles made with rice jelly, coconut milk and palm sugar. *Nam khao* consists of crispy rice balls added to a salad – with coconut, sausages, peanuts, red onions, herbs, red chilli peppers, shallots and limes – that is eaten in a lettuce wrap. The batter of *kanom dok bua*, lotus flower cookies, is made from coconut milk and is deep-fried. *Kanom dok bua* is similar to a flower-like sweet popular in South India.

Many traditional foods in Indonesia are coconut based, prepared with *bongo dilangato* (freshly grated coconut), *hulango bongo* (coconut milk) or *yinulo* (home-made coconut oil). On the island of Java, images carved in Buddhist temple reliefs at the UNESCO World Heritage site of Borobudur, dating to the ninth century CE, show figures picking coconuts from trees. Among the carvings, there is a relief of an important scene depicting Sujata offering *kiribath*, a traditional dish of rice cooked with coconut milk, to the Buddha after his period of meditation. This same scene is depicted on walls of temples in Cambodia and Myanmar, illustrating the deep significance of this coconut milk-based dish to Buddhists.

On the Indonesian island of Bali, coconut plays a significant role in Balinese Hindu religion, a minority faith in this, the most populous Muslim country in the world. The preparation of ceremonial food and offerings is in itself a religious act of worship and an important way of honouring the multitude of gods. Large ceremonial feasts that include dishes featuring coconut are held regularly and require considerable time and expense, which is shared by the community.

Reliefs showing coconut palms at Borobudur, 9th century CE.

Lawar, which translates as 'thinly sliced', is the most famous and highly perishable religious ritual festival food in Bali. It uses coconut and is traditionally made by men under the leadership of male culinary specialists. Coconut moonshine, *arak*, flows freely during the long hours required of the preparation for the feast, increasing the male communal camaraderie. The long night of rhythmic chopping of ingredients and of breaking open and grating the coconuts is an integral part of the ritual food preparations. Women are allowed to wash salad ingredients, fry onions, prepare the rice and vegetables, provide refreshments for guests and assemble the elaborately beautiful coconut leaf offerings that are integral to the ceremonies. Preparation methods require fresh, shaved and roasted coconut and seasoned coconut milk, along with many other vegetable and meat ingredients. Essential for a ritual *lawar* is fresh congealed pig's blood and the finely minced cooked innards of sacrificial animals. There are five

Balinese offerings made of coconut leaves.

types of *lawar*, named by their colour and representing the five directions, all containing the common ingredient of roasted coconut. White *lawar* is prepared with coconut meat and chicken, and there are recipes for vegetarian *lawar* that use only coconut. For other ritual dishes, turmeric is used to dye the grated coconut a vivid yellow.[4]

In Bali, coconut leaves are an important component of daily offerings, as well as special ceremonial celebrations. *Sajeng* (or *sajen*) are six 20-centimetre (8 in.) offering trays that are constructed of coconut leaves and filled with a few grains of rice, flowers, salt and chilli peppers, and placed by the women of the household at specific locations in the

Bali traditional painting with coconut palms.

compound to placate evil spirits and negative forces.[5] Balinese tradition links the coconut palm to fertility. When a child is born, the parents place the placenta in a coconut shell and hang it from a tree in the family compound.[6] Another tradition in Bali is to give newborn babies coconut water just after birth.

Known as the 'king of Indonesian dishes', beef *rendang* – beef or buffalo cooked for hours in coconut milk and spices – was voted number one in a 2017 CNN survey of the fifty most delicious foods in the world.[7] Making *rendang* is known as *marandang*, which is an exercise in the lessons of patience, wisdom and persistence. Originating with the Minangkabau people, who live in the highlands of the island of West Sumatra in Indonesia, the four ingredients of the dish are said to represent characteristics of the Minangkabau people. The meat symbolizes the revered elders, and the coconut milk refers to the intellectuals of the community, including the teachers, poets and writers. The heat of the chilli symbolizes religious leaders and Sharia law. The spices must include lemongrass, galangal and coriander, but there are countless additions and variations that represent the total society, with all its diversity, and the necessity to keep a balance for the community to thrive.[8] Other coconut-based dishes found throughout Indonesia include *rawon kluwek*, a black coconut soup, and *dadar gulung*, stunningly green pancake rolls stuffed with grated coconut.[9]

A form of satay – small pieces of grilled meat served in a sauce – popular in Bali, *sate lilit* is made with ground meat that is combined with grated coconut and then grilled on a fire of coconut husks. The midrib of the coconut palm frond is traditionally used as a skewer for satay. An entire street food area in Singapore is devoted in the evenings to a Malay version of satay. Chicken or beef is marinated and then skewered and grilled, accompanied by a peanut sauce that often can include coconut.

Peranakan cuisine is another culinary tradition that developed through migrating populations and makes liberal use of coconut, particularly in the spicy noodle soup known as *laksa*. Peranakan culture refers to descendants of Chinese merchants who traded in the nineteenth century and eventually settled throughout the Southeast Asian port cities of Penang, Medan, Malacca, Palembang, Batavia (Jakarta) and Singapore, marrying local women. Peranakan wives invented *laksa*, which derives from a Hokkien word meaning 'spicy sand', by adding local ingredients, including coconut, to various noodle soup dishes from further north to please their Chinese husbands, resulting in a fusion culinary tradition that is alive and well today. Within the many variations, Singapore *laksa* is most defined by creamy coconut.

It is difficult to imagine the dense city-state of Singapore as a location for coconut plantations, but in the nineteenth century, a large portion of the land was held for this valuable crop, which was exported for copra. Today, in the pristinely landscaped environment, coconut palms are occasionally used as ornamentals, but coconuts are not allowed to grow and drop randomly, and possibly dangerously, on people or cars. Because of their unique history as citizens of a critical centre of commerce, Singaporeans enjoy a famously expansive international food scene, including Peranakan, Malay, Indian and European cuisines.

Kaya jam is a Malaysian invention that is a popular breakfast option in Singapore and is made with coconut, eggs and caramel. The word *kaya* in Malay language means 'rich', and this spread is the epitome of rich.

Pulut inti, a popular sweet at Singaporean celebrations and weddings, is a traditional Malaysian *kuih*, a dessert often

Singaporean *laksa.*

shaped into small pyramids and wrapped in banana leaves, made of steamed glutinous rice with a sweet, shredded coconut topping. Adopted into Peranakan cuisine, the rice may be coloured a beautiful pale blue using the natural dyeing properties of *bunga telang*, the blue pea flower. In the Little India neighbourhood of Singapore, it is possible to find endless South Indian curries with rich coconut bases or to purchase a fresh coconut to sip while in the intense heat and humidity. One can also observe traditional uses of coconuts in Hindu religious ceremonies.

Beloved by Singaporeans, *nasi lemak* is considered the de facto national dish of Malaysia. Rich coconut milk rice is

Singapore and Malay *pulut inti.*

sometimes flavoured with pandan, served with *sambal* (chilli sauce or paste), fried crispy anchovies, toasted peanuts and cucumber, and garnished with hard-boiled egg or tomatoes. The Nasi Lemak Project in Malaysia aims to identify poor urban families and teach them how to make a living selling *nasi lemak*, and to develop the skills and knowledge needed to set up a small business, including accounting, supplies and logistics.

Coconut does not immediately come to mind when thinking of Chinese cuisine, but there is evidence that as early as the Tang dynasty (618–907 CE), the Chinese valued the coconut in much the same way as medieval Europeans: as a beautiful material to carve and embellish with precious metals such as silver. In Hainan province, the skill of carving coconut shells has been designated a part of the province's National

Intangible Cultural Heritage. Delicately designed coconut sculptures continue to be created today as both souvenirs and works of art. Master carvers from Hainan have visited their counterparts in the Seychelles to share techniques and knowledge.[10]

Known as 'the Kingdom of Coconuts' or 'Coconut Island', Hainan Island in the South China Sea grows 99 per cent of all coconuts in China. There are numerous legends relating to the origin of the coconut tree from this area. One tells of a woman in ancient times who waited in vain on the beach for her seafaring husband to return. She gradually turned into the coconut tree herself, its leaves serving as her hat.[11] A happier love-linked legend describes the interplanted coconut and areca (betel nut) palms as entwined lovers.

On Hainan Island, there is a popular annual international coconut festival which lasts for ten days and begins around the third day of the third lunar month. In Haikou City, streets are lined with coconut oil lamps and coconut-based products and foods are celebrated everywhere.

Coconut rice, or 'coconut boats', are a local coconut speciality in Hainan; they are made by drilling a hole in the top of a coconut. Glutinous rice and sweet, grated coconut meat are put into the hole; the coconut is boiled for several hours, and then cracked open and eaten as a dessert shaped like a small boat.

Like coconut rice, a coconut soup is also made and served in the shell of a coconut. Slowly cooked over several hours, the coconut meat absorbs the herbs and other ingredients, which can include chicken and ginseng, or pigeons with black mushrooms and lotus seeds.[12]

A coconut liquor made in Hainan as early as the Song dynasty (960–1279) has a relatively low alcohol content, allowing the coconut flavour to stand out. Many coconut sweets are available in Hainan, as well as coconut buns, and *yi bua*, a Hainanese sweet, which has rice-flour skin and a filling of shredded coconut, ground peanuts, *gula melaka* (palm sugar with a caramel taste like brown sugar), sesame seeds, ginger and dried persimmons.

Dried and sweetened coconut is a must on every Chinese New Year Tray of Togetherness. The sugared coconut ribbons in the round or eight-sided tray symbolize togetherness, based on the meaning of the Cantonese word *ye zi*, which sounds similar to the words for 'grandfather' and 'grandson', and expresses the Confucian desire for strong family unity and respect through generations.

One of the most famous regional specialities on the island of Hainan is *Wenchang* chicken, thought by many to be among the best chicken dishes in all Chinese cuisine. There is even a popular saying in Hainan, 'No Wenchang chicken, no banquet.' True *Wenchang* chicken is prepared with chicken raised in Hainan and fed with banyan seeds for nine months before it is 'confined in a basket in a quiet location away from light'.[13] Ground peanut cake, shredded coconut flesh, water caltrop, heated cooked rice and other fattening foods are then fed to the chicken. As populations migrated from Hainan to other parts of Southeast Asia, they brought with them a preference for this chicken, which evolved into a dish popular in all countries in Southeast Asia and named after their province, Hainanese chicken rice.

More widely in China, traditional medicine classifies all foods as either warming or cooling, and the goal is to obtain a perfect balance to optimize a healthy body. Coconut is noted as 'cooling', a quality that serves well, as it is used to moderate spicy curries in Thailand and South India.

China has also not been left behind in the current coconut water health craze, but as in other countries, advertisers' claims can go too far. One Chinese coconut water manufacturer was censured when it used photographs of well-endowed women in wet T-shirts for promotional campaigns that promised that drinking coconut water would make a woman's breasts grow bigger.[14]

Covered coconut cup mounted in pewter and carved with a poem and scenes of ships, 1836.

4
South Asia

In Point de Gall I did grow on a tree so high
A black man cut me down
A sailor did me buy
My blood he drank
My flesh did eat
My raiment hove away
And here remains my ribs and trucks
Until this very day[1]

A poem carved into the coconut shell which is mounted in silver as a cup and today resides in the Winterthur Museum, Garden & Library collection of the Du Pont family speaks to the essential importance of coconut. The narrator is the coconut itself, describing its life cycle from vital human sustenance to a valuable and enduring collectible artefact. 'Point de Gall' is a reference to the port at Pont de Gall in Sri Lanka. At the time of the poem's inscription in 1836, Sri Lanka was a colony of the United Kingdom and an important coconut export region for trading ships.

Worldwide there are many agencies, both governmental and non-governmental, that deal with various agricultural products, but only one country has a minister appointed specifically to oversee the coconut's continued success both at home and as an export abroad. Coconut is considered to be so important to the current well-being of the people of Sri Lanka that the Minister of Coconut has been a cabinet-level position since 1976. There is a variety of coconut native to Sri Lanka that is a vivid yellow colour called king coconut, or *thembili*. A young king coconut contains especially sweet juice for drinking. Producers are beginning to emphasize this in marketing the juice for export.

While India, the world's third-largest producer of coconut, may not have a specific minister of coconut, the government created a Coconut Development Board in 1981 and established a coconut museum, which is part of the Department of Agriculture Development & Farmers' Welfare, in Kochi, Kerala. The Indian government has also founded a training organization called Friends of Coconut Tree (FOCT) to help solve the problem of the shortage of coconut tree climbers. The goal is to train 5,000 unemployed young people in palm climbing and other technical skills related to coconut farming. In 2018 the Bishop Kurialacherry College for Women in Amalagiri launched a course in coconut tree climbing and harvesting for its female students, which, considering India's strictly defined gender roles, is evidence of the importance of the coconut industry to the nation and the severity of the skilled labour shortage.

The importance of the coconut is deeply rooted in Indian culture. According to the Hindu religious text Vishnu Purana, the creation of the coconut palm involved a violent power struggle between gods and man – and of course, a woman was involved as well. A famous sage named Viśvāmitra, who had attained superhuman powers, owed a favour to his mortal friend King Trishanku, who had been exiled by his own father for misbehaviour with a woman. King Trishanku wanted to be raised to the heaven of the gods in his mortal form, and Viśvāmitra complied. The powerful god Indra, along with all the sages and gods, were angered and insulted by the audacity of Viśvāmitra and hurled the mortal king back to earth. Using his superhuman powers, Viśvāmitra halted the king's fall in mid-air and supported him with a pole, which became the coconut palm. King Trishanku's head became the coconut fruit, his beard and hair becoming its husk.[2]

The coconut palm is *Kalpavriksha*, a term referring to the wish-fulfilling capacity that makes the tree sacred to Hindus and the purest form of offering to the gods. *Kalpavriksha* is also the name of a programme sponsored by Marico, a company in India that aims to help traditional farmers increase their incomes by raising coconut yields through pest control practices and nutrient-management technologies.[3]

There are coconut references in the early Sanskrit texts the Mahabharata, the Ramayana and the Puranas. The sage Viśvāmitra is credited with replacing the cruel ritual of sacrificing a human or animal head with a coconut in Hindu ceremonies. The round shape and eyes of the coconut serve as a symbol of the human head offering. From the time of the Agni Purana and the Brahma Purana (800–900 CE), the coconut became a required part of virtually every Hindu *puja* ritual and festival. This practice continues today.

The breaking of a coconut in such rituals is a metaphor for destroying the tough, hard shell of the human ego. The rough, fibrous exterior represents the worst in humankind: jealousy, greed, lust and selfishness, which must be stripped away. The soft white flesh of the inner coconut represents inner light and beauty. Breaking or smashing the coconut in a ceremony suggests surrendering or transcending the ego and connecting with divine essence, a desire to break through negative thoughts and be awakened. There are several festivals

Breaking a coconut at a Hindu temple, Kerala, India.

in India during which masses of devotees have coconuts broken on their heads by temple priests.

The three marks on the coconut symbolize the trinity of the most important Hindu deities: Brahma the creator, Vishnu the preserver and Shiva the destroyer. Coconuts and bananas are gifts from the goddess Lakshmi, and she is often illustrated holding a coconut. Before beginning a task or journey, a Hindu might smash a coconut in the temple to summon the assistance of the elephant-headed Lord Ganesha, remover of obstacles. As prasadam or prasad, blessed or holy food, the coconut pieces are distributed to devotees after the worship service is completed.

The coconut is an important element in Indian rites of passage ceremonies, from naming babies to weddings and even in death, in which the human head may be represented by a coconut in the cremation ceremony if there is no body.[4] Coconuts are exchanged as symbols of fertility, good luck and prosperity in Hindu weddings. In South India, highly embellished wedding coconuts, beaded and bejewelled, are carried by the bride as she makes her way to the wedding canopy. Leaves of the coconut palm may be woven into elaborate decorations for weddings and special social and religious functions. To ensure wealth and act as a witness to a traditional Hindu wedding, the unopened inflorescence, or flower bud, of the coconut is placed in a rice-filled *para*, a wooden container that is used by farmers to measure rice.[5]

Food for a wedding banquet is lavish and, especially in South India, will include dishes, such as prawn *malabar*, that are coconut based. A dish originating in Kerala and popular for weddings as well as for other celebrations is *shakara payasam*. Traditionally a *payasam*, or *prathaman*, dish is made by boiling rice with coconut milk, sugar and spices into a thick pudding, and then served on a plantain leaf at the end of a Sadya.

A Sadya, meaning 'banquet' in Malayalam, the language of the state of Kerala, is an extravagant vegetarian feast of specific dishes traditionally laid out in a specific order on a banana leaf. The feast could include up to 28 dishes, or, for a very special occasion, up to 64 items, many of which include coconut as a main ingredient, are cooked in coconut milk or are fried in coconut oil.

In 2009 a Guinness World Record was set for the largest annual gathering of women anywhere in the world, at a temple in Kerala, where 2.5 million women had assembled to cook at the Attukal Pongala, a religious festival celebrated at the

Coconut wedding decorations, Mumbai, India.

Sadya, a special meal in Kerala, India, served on banana leaves.

Attukal Bhagavathy Temple in Thiruvananthapuram. The devout women were cooking divine food to appease the goddess of the temple: a *payasam* made from rice, jaggery, coconut and plantains. The women had travelled for miles to participate and brought along their own cooking pots and coconut husks, which served as fuel for cooking.[6]

Avial or *aviyal*, translated as 'mixture', is a popular dish from Tamil Nadu made of mixed vegetables, coconut and milk curd, whose history draws on an episode in the Hindu epic Mahabharata. Bhima, one of the five Pandava brothers, was thought to have drowned, and a great ceremonial funeral feast was planned for him. But the hero miraculously returned. Rather than waste the preparations, Bhima, who had disguised himself as a cook, offered to mix all the ingredients with coconut milk, creating *aviyal*.[7] Another story about the creation of this dish credits the king of Travancore, who offered a grand feast to all his subjects. Since his staff underestimated the crowd, the food ran out, and the king was able to save the day by having his cook collect all the scraps and cook them in coconut milk.

One of the most dramatic culinary scenes imaginable occurs once a year when Mumbai's *masalawaalis* (spice merchants) roast and pound sometimes more than thirty ingredients, including dried coconut, to create 'bottle' masala spice mixtures from old family recipes. This annual event is a unique tradition among a small Christian community of East India, who settled in what is today Mumbai. 'Bottle' refers to the original practice of storing the roasted spice blend in old beer bottles, whose amber colour protected the product from the sun. *Masalawaalis* used to travel from home to home selling their bottles, but today crowds of women assemble at the Mumbai spice markets to choose their ingredients and have them pounded and roasted to their individual orders.[8]

The state of Kerala in South India is known as the 'land of coconuts'. The Malayalam word *kera* means 'coconut tree', and *lam*, 'land'. Coconut palms grow abundantly along the coast and the backwaters. The cuisine of the region is heavily coconut based. Coconut is used in many ways: sliced, baked, grated, ground into a paste. Coconut oil is used in cooking, and coconut husks and charcoal from coconut shells are the traditional fuels. Most of the many curries which form the mainstay of the traditional daily meal in Kerala are coconut based, including *theeyal* and *aviyal*.

Puttu is a steamed cake-like delicacy popular for breakfast in Kerala. A mixture of rice powder is combined with coconut and pressed into a cylinder, previously a hollow bamboo tube, but now a special kitchen utensil called the *puttikutti*. Many meals include a *thoran*, a dry vegetable and coconut dish which can be made of any available chopped leafy vegetables, which are then combined with grated coconut. *Olan* is a coconut-milk-based vegetable stew essential to the Sadya feast in Kerala; it is made with pumpkin or ash gourd and black-eyed peas. Many coconut-based foods popular in Kerala and Tamil Nadu in South India have found their way to neighbouring Sri Lanka.

More than 70 per cent of the Sri Lankan population is Buddhist. The coconut has a prominent role in Buddhist

Masala making in Mumbai, India.

traditions and rituals. Lighting lamps using coconut oil – symbolizing the enlightenment of Buddha, the light of knowledge contrasting with the darkness of evil – is an essential part of the worship of the Bodhi Tree, under which Buddha became enlightened. Flowers and coconut oil are indispensable in Buddhist worship offerings, and coconut oil is strictly prepared to be as pure as possible. The Vesak festival celebrating the birth, life and the release from cycles of rebirth known as *parinirvana* of Buddha is a festival of light calling for thousands of coconut lamps. *Kiribat*, or *kiribath*, a coconut-milk rice dish formed into a cake and cut into diamond shapes, is a food offering placed before the Buddha. A significant episode in Buddha's life often depicted in temple murals involves a woman named Sujata offering *kiribat* to him just before he attains enlightenment.[9]

Kiribat – *kiri*, meaning 'milk', and *bath* or *bat*, meaning 'rice' – is still an important food prepared to celebrate religious rituals, rites of passage and special occasions in the Sinhalese home. This simple coconut rice dish, having a consistency similar to risotto, is the first solid food fed to infants when they are weaned from breast milk. A single grain of rice is placed on the baby's lips at a special ceremony with the family in a Buddhist temple. Traditionally, *kiribat* must be consumed as the first meal of a new year, following a particular ritual. The dish is made in a new clay pot for the occasion. The head of the family arranges members to be facing in prescribed auspicious directions and feeds each person a single bite at a pre-determined propitious time. During new year celebrations, this ritual is followed by a sweet feast of treats, many of which are coconut based.[10]

At weddings, *kiribat* is fed by bridegrooms to their brides. Rice and coconut milk, the basic foods of Sri Lankan cuisine, symbolize prosperity, good luck and good fortune. Another

Statue of Sujata offering *kiribath* to the Buddha, Kandy, Sri Lanka.

Sri Lankan wedding tradition requires an uncle or other male member of the bride's family to break a coconut during the ceremony. One explanation for this ritual is that it is bad luck for guests to see the bridal couple as they step down from the platform on which the wedding ceremony is held, so the loud noise of the breaking coconut would distract the guests.[11]

Temple ceremony for a baby in India. The baby is being fed coconut as its first food.

Coconut is grown on about 20 to 25 per cent of Sri Lanka's arable land, and more than 1,350,000 Sri Lankans are employed in the production, processing and commercial sides.[12] More than 75 per cent of coconuts produced are consumed locally, and coconut palms are protected by the government. Cutting young coconut trees is illegal.

A meal without coconut as an ingredient is practically unimaginable to Sri Lankans. Coconut and coconut milk are included in curries, salads and sweets. *Pol sambol*, a spicy dry coconut chutney, is a popular condiment made with freshly grated coconut.

A hopper or *appam* is a very thin bowl-shaped pancake, popular in Sri Lanka but originating in South India. When the batter is made with coconut milk, it is called a milk hopper. The batter will have a leavening agent which might also be coconut toddy. String hoppers (*idiyappam*) require a similar rice flour batter, which is squeezed into a sort of sieve, producing a thin noodle. The Tamil word *idi* means 'broken down', and *appam* means 'pancake'; string hoppers are often eaten at breakfast with a curry. In Karnataka, string hoppers are served with a coconut milk dessert dish called *rasayana*, which combines

Exchanging *kiribath* at the wedding ceremony of Damayanthi Werapitiya in Kandy, Sri Lanka.

the milk with various fruits. Surprisingly, in London, hoppers and string hoppers are becoming a popular pub food.

Achcharu, also called *acar* (Malay pickle) is a popular accompaniment to a main dish. It is made with coconut vinegar and contains mixed chopped vegetables in a combination of sweet, sour and spicy pickled sauce. Sri Lankan cuisine was influenced by both Dutch and Indonesian food traditions because of Sri Lanka's location along trade routes during the

Hoppers with king coconut in Sri Lanka.

Marianne North, *Cocoanut Palms on the Coast near Galle, Ceylon*, 1876, oil on canvas.

colonial period. Malay *achcharu* originated in the minority Malay community, descending from those who came to live in Sri Lanka during Dutch and British rule.

Sweets are recognized as a culinary art form in Sri Lanka. Egg and butter sweets came about through Dutch and Portuguese influences. *Watalappam*, a coconut custard made with jaggery or palm sugar, cashew nuts, cardamom, cloves and nutmeg, is a classic dessert among all Sri Lankans found at weddings and celebrations and particularly popular among Sri Lankan Muslims during Ramadan. The name evolved from a combination of Tamil words – *vattil* (cup) and *appam* (pancake) – with a Dutch word, *vla*, meaning 'custard'.[13] *Kokis*, of Dutch origin, are made with a fried rice and coconut milk batter in the shape of stars or flowers, and they are especially popular at new year celebrations.

Aluwa is made with coconut treacle (syrup made from sap) and rice flour, and served at cultural festivals as a representative Sri Lankan sweet. A much more difficult sweet to prepare, more often purchased from sweet shops, *aasmi* is made from a rice flour and coconut milk batter that traditionally would be poured through a coconut shell that had been punctured with small holes. This results in a web-like design on the hot oil that is similar to string *hoppers* in appearance. *Pani pol* are crêpes stuffed with a coconut jaggery filling.

Victorian botanical painter Marianne North spent several weeks in Sri Lanka (Ceylon) documenting trees and flowers, and remarked in her autobiography, *Recollections of a Happy Life*, 'The cocoa-nuts, with their endless variety of curves, were always a marvel to me, how they kept their balance, with their heavy heads and slender trunks leaning over the golden sand, and within a few yards of the pure clear sea waves.'[14] North was a fan of coconut water as well, noting that the coconut 'is filled with a liquor clear as water, cool and better flavoured than wine or any other kind of drink whatever'.[15]

5
The South Pacific and the Philippines

In various tales from Polynesian mythology, the hero of the coconut origin story, known sometimes as Maui, saves a damsel in distress by beheading an evil character or monster. The coconut palm sprouts from the buried head of the dead creature. Maui is variously a trickster, a fool or a hero who uses trickery to triumph over forces of evil.[1] He is the male lead character in Disney's 2016 film *Moana*, in which the film-makers incorporated myths from the South Pacific. The heroine, Moana, is urged to consider the virtues of the coconut on her lovely island.

While mention of the South Pacific conjures up an image of the beach, the ocean and coconut palms, rarely does that image include food. The odd tropical drink appears in the scene. But how was, and is, coconut consumed in this area where it grows easily? As would be expected on tropical islands, many kinds of fish are prepared with a coconut sauce. When he was ill with fever and congested lungs on the island of Tahiti, the author of the adventure novel *Treasure Island*, Robert Louis Stevenson, was nursed back to health by a local princess, Moe. She fed him a dish of mullet soaked in brine with a sauce of coconut milk, lime and pepper several times a day.

Spanish Christian missionaries first arrived in the South Pacific in the 1660s, sailing from their base in the Philippines. The first permanent mission in the region was established by the British in 1797. Several theologians from the Pacific Island region have compared the traditional pre-Christian Polynesian kava ceremony to the Christian Eucharist. The kava ceremony involves the preparation and communal sharing of a unique beverage which is made from the roots of a kava bush. Once a traditional religious ceremony, the kava ceremony is now more often performed as a welcome ceremony for visitors and tourists. The preparation involves participants chewing the fibres of kava and mixing it with their own spit to make a liquid, which is served in half-coconut shells called kava cups. Coconut may be eaten as part of the ceremony as well. Particularly in Samoa, the ritual has retained significance and has been incorporated into the Catholic Mass, where kava has replaced the wine of the service.[2]

While coconut and the coconut palm are not specifically mentioned in the Bible, a Pacific Island-based interpretation of Christianity known as coconut theology links the coconut to the most significant meal in Christianity, the Last Supper. Developed by Doctor Sione 'Amanaki Havea, a theologian from Tonga, in 1986, coconut theology suggests that the Pacific region's indigenous plants and resources could be used symbolically to help people of the region better understand elements of the Christian doctrine. Reverend Piula Alailima, pastor of Wesley Methodist Church in Honolulu, notes, 'When we break the body of the coconut and partake of the juice, it's a symbol of the body and blood of Christ, of sacrifice, of community and the common good.'[3]

One of the most famous residents of Tahiti, Paul Gauguin, included coconut palms in many of the vibrant coloured scenes

Paul Gauguin, *The Meal*, 1891, oil on paper glued on canvas.

he painted of the island. One of the earliest paintings the artist completed when he first arrived is titled *The Meal.* The painting portrays a strangely staged composition depicting three puzzled-looking children sitting uneasily facing a tablescape of bananas, guavas, oranges and a large wooden bowl containing coconut milk. There are also several small sketches by Gauguin of scenes in Tahiti, which he designed to illustrate the menus for dinner parties he hosted in 1900. One of these drawings is a lovely rendering of a coconut palm, along with the list of food to be served. The fare for the evening included chicken with 'sauce coco', combining French and Tahitian fare. Other than the banquet menus, there is no written documentation of what Gauguin might have eaten during his years in Tahiti. It is likely he would have eaten a traditional Tahitian fish dish, *e'ia ota* or *poisson cru*, which is lime-marinated fish cooked with coconut milk.[4]

Demonstrating the many traditional uses of coconut. Polynesian Cultural Center, Oahu, Hawaii.

Thirty years later, when visiting Tahiti, the French painter Henri Matisse wrote to his wife that he was delighted to be treated to a *ma'a Tahiti*, a traditional feast, in which he enjoyed eating cooked breadfruit in coconut milk with his fingers, and especially liked the coconut milk and curry sauce.[5]

In Samoa, a simple sweet of mashed bananas with coconut cream is popular. Much more complicated is the preparation of *palusami*, coconut cream and onion wrapped in taro leaves and prepared in the *umu*, a sort of oven placed on the ground, which uses hot lava rocks to cook the food. This process is traditionally handled by the men of the island.

The same type of oven is traditional in Hawaii, where coconut water is called *noelani*, meaning 'dew from the heavens'. An iconic symbol of Hawaii, the coconut palm was brought to the islands by early migrations in prehistoric times. A well-known legend describes the coconut tree as a path or bridge to another world: a young Hawaiian boy longs for his father, who has returned to his homeland of Tahiti. His mother, Hina, sings a plea for her son: 'O life giving coconut of Tahiti, o far-traveling coconut', and a coconut palm miraculously appears. The boy climbs the palm tree, which bends and stretches all the way to Tahiti, where he is reunited with his father.[6]

McDonald's *haupia*-filled pie.

Though taro and breadfruit comprise the basics of the Hawaiian diet, there are many coconut dishes as well. *Haupia* is a white, gelatinous, coconut-milk-based pudding, which is used as a filling or topping, or eaten alone. *Haupia* is often used as a topping or filling between layers on wedding cakes. McDonald's offers a *haupia*-filled fried pie on its menus in Hawaii. *Pani popo*, also popular in Hawaii and Samoa, is a rich treat made with both sweetened condensed milk and coconut milk poured over sweet dinner rolls.

The cookbook *I Am a Filipino: And This Is How We Cook* by Nicole Ponseca (the CEO and chef at Maharlika and Jeepney restaurants in New York City) and chef Miguel Trinidad was named by the *New York Times* as one of the best cookbooks of 2018, among other prestigious culinary awards. Filipino food is finally being recognized internationally as a unique cuisine, and coconut is one of the most essential ingredients. The Filipino culinary tradition combines elements of both Southeast Asia and South Pacific cuisine, with dishes from its Spanish colonial history. As the world's second-largest producer of coconuts, for the Philippines, the coconut is an economically important crop for both home use and export. More than 25 million Filipinos depend directly or indirectly on the coconut industry for their livelihoods. But, as in many other countries, the Philippines is struggling with problems of climate change; older, less productive coconut trees; diseases and pests; and changes in the labour force. In the face of this, the government and trade organizations are making efforts to increase innovation and production through research initiatives and technological assistance to farmers.

Coconut is used in food preparations in many creative and unusual ways in the Philippines. *Latik*, or coconut curds, for example, is a by-product of the process of making coconut oil

Latik coconut curds, the Philippines.

and is sprinkled on sweet desserts or added to salads for texture and sweetness. *Latik* curds are used as a topping for *tibok tibok*, which translates as 'heartbeat', a dessert pudding made of carabao (water buffalo) milk, with a soft gelatine-like texture. Its name refers to the rhythmic plopping sound made as the batter thickens on the stove. The surface of the batter appears to literally pulsate.

Coconut vinegar is part of the Filipino flavour palette and a component of many varieties of the famous Filipino dish *adobo*. *Balut*, meaning 'wrapped', is a fertilized bird embryo, often that of a duck, that is boiled and then consumed from its shell. It is considered an aphrodisiac. *Balut* is often served with a sauce of coconut vinegar, which some foodies think could be the next big coconut product.

Macapuno (or *makapuno*) is the jelly-like flesh of a naturally occurring but rare coconut variant, found in about one in every one hundred coconuts. It was first identified as a desirable culinary ingredient in the Philippines in the 1930s and has since become a traditional delicacy. At a recent coconut festival in Toronto, Canada, where there is a sizeable expatriate Filipino community, the Philippine Trade Forum launched

Ube-macapuno cake, the Philippines.

a 'Macapuno Breakthrough Program', the goal being to encourage overseas Filipino investors to support a project to develop Alabat Island, Quezon, where there is a population of poor farmers, into a unique location for the growth of these high-value *macapuno* coconut palms.[7] *Macapuno* is used in traditional sweets such as halo-halo and when combined with another favourite Philippine ingredient, *ube halaya* (mashed purple yam), results in a stunning *ube-macapuno* cake. *Ube-macapuno*-flavoured ice cream is a popular flavour throughout the Philippines.

The Philippines is famous for its many festivals, both religious and secular. The San Pablo Coconut Festival is held every 15 January and celebrates all things coconut, with street dancing and a parade with floats. The Coco Carnival Queen candidates compete in costumes made from coconut, while honouring the city's patron, St Paul the Hermit. San Pablo City is home to the Franklin Baker Company of the Philippines, one of the country's largest coconut-processing facilities, and many families in the area are involved in coconut production.

The Barugo Sanggutan Festival is a blend of religion, tradition, animism and pure fun. This celebration honours the process of making *bahalina*, which has an alcohol content of 10 to 13 per cent, from *tuba* (an alcoholic drink made from coconut palm sap) that has been aged for several months or even several years. To make this red wine, the sap of the coconut buds is collected and then fermented. *Lambanog* is another liquor distilled from *tuba*, but with a higher alcohol content of 40 to 45 per cent.

The term *guinataan* describes coconut-milk-based dishes – *gata* is the Tagalog word for 'coconut'. *Kakanin* is a term for sweets made with both glutinous rice and coconut cream or milk. *Puto* are Filipino steamed rice cakes that are prepared with a rice dough that is fermented by *tuba*, as a form of

Making their famous *buko* pie in Colette's factory, San Pablo City, the Philippines.

yeast, in a similar way as the dough for *Bibingka.* Both are popular street foods during the Christmas season. *Binignit* is a coconut-milk-based meatless soup prepared for the Christian Holy Week and eaten on Good Friday. Ingredients include tubers, jackfruit strips, sago and glutinous rice.

Lumpiang or *lumpiang ubod* is a type of 'Filipino spring roll', which likely evolved from a dish brought by Chinese traders who began calling into Filipino ports in the ninth century. The deep-fried roll is made with strips of coconut palm hearts and the fibrous pith from the inner core and growing bud of the coconut palm. Removing the *ubod* (heart of coconut palm) actually kills the coconut palm, so the *ubod* is almost always acquired from fallen coconut trees or trees that are being cut down for thinning.

Buko pie is a popular coconut dessert originating in the province of Laguna, on the island of Luzon in the Philippines, and is a favourite food gift souvenir, or *pasalubong*, meaning 'bring home something for me'. *Buko* is the Tagalog word for 'young coconut', and the pie consists of strips of fresh, tender young coconut meat in a creamy filling, which includes coconut milk and sweetened condensed milk, with a flaky pie crust. Everyone agrees that the origin of the idea for pie was the brainchild of the Pahud sisters, one of whom had worked in the United States and had learned how to make American apple pie. Back home in the Philippines in 1965, the sisters developed their dessert using coconuts rather than apples. Today there is fierce competition to produce the best *buko* pie among the three major producers in the Laguna area. Orient, Colette's and Lety's are the most prominent, and more than twenty other producers offer their own variations today. Exporting this beloved treat to overseas Filipinos and foreign markets has been a challenge, and makers are experimenting with preservation techniques such as blast freezing.[8] Filipino cuisine is gaining popularity worldwide as more and more products make their way into shops beyond Filipino speciality stores.

Stained-glass window of Moses and the Burning Bush with coconut palms in the background, designed by Benjamin Shoemaker in 1873 for the Masonic Temple in Philadelphia.

6
Africa and the Middle East

'Only the man who is not hungry
says the coconut has a hard shell.'
Malawian proverb

The artist Benjamin Shoemaker, who created a stained-glass window for the grand Masonic Temple in Philadelphia in 1873, must have been influenced by the romance and exoticism of coconuts as he placed Moses and the burning bush below what is clearly a coconut tree in the Holy Land. Visions of palm trees do come to mind when imagining the Middle East, but those would more accurately be date palms, not coconut palms. Exceptions are found in the microclimate along the coast of Oman, the Dhofar region surrounding the city of Salalah, and Yemen's Al Mahrah and Hadhramaut Governates, where coconut palms flourish. In addition to the favourable coastal climate, these areas had historical maritime commercial ties with India and China as well as Myanmar (Burma), Malaysia, Indonesia and their close neighbours in East Africa.

From the seat of his empire in Kabul, Afghanistan, far from Oman and the Arabian Sea coast, the Mughal emperor Babur (1483–1530) included the coconut palm and coconut in his memoirs, the *Baburnama* or *Letters of Babur*. Illustrated editions include beautiful colour plates depicting the coconut palms with birds. Babur notes of the coconut water, 'it tastes well and is very often drunk in summer, mixed with sugar.'[1] A sherbet recipe from the Mughal court manuscript *Ni'matnama* or *Book of Delights* calls for minced coconut, mangoes, fresh ginger, onions, lime juice, cardamom, cloves, pepper, turmeric, fenugreek and asafoetida.[2] Babur confirms earlier descriptions of the importance of coconut in the process of obtaining luxury foods through trade: 'cordage of all the ships and boats of the rivers are made of this outer covering of the coconut.'[3]

Coir rope produced from coconut husks was used in Oman for constructing traditional seagoing dhow ships, which were assembled without nails, technology which may have been learned from trading partners in India, where coconuts had been cultivated for hundreds of years. Ibn Battuta describes these vessels sewn together with coir as *jalbah* in his writings in the years 1325–54 and remarks on the presence of what is called the 'Indian nut' in *zaatar*, a popular spice mix.[4]

After the rise of Islam in the seventh century, powerful Arab empires traded along the maritime spice route. As a result of the spice trade that moved through Oman from India and beyond, there are many Omani recipes that incorporate Indian spices such as cumin, coriander, turmeric, cinnamon and cloves. *Kuku paka*, a chicken coconut curry, suggests Indian roots because of the spices it contains.[5] In order to survive long ocean journeys, coconut milk from East Africa was powdered for a much longer shelf life.

Desserts and confections containing coconut are popular throughout the Middle East and are enjoyed as part of the celebration of the end of the Ramadan fast. *Qashat al-narjeel* is a traditional Omani coconut cookie made of just three ingredients: shredded coconut, powdered milk and sugar. It

Folio of the Mughal-dynasty *Baburnama*, depicting birds in a coconut grove (1588).

resembles a crispy white bark and is often served with tea or coffee. Another confection called *chaklama* is similar to a macaroon but has added cardamom flavouring.[6]

In Egypt, *sobia* is a popular drink enjoyed especially during Iftar, the month of Ramadan. It is served chilled and made with coconut milk as a base and flavoured variously with tamarind, cardamom and cinnamon, and garnished with raisins, pistachios or rose petals. *Sobia* is also a Koranic girl's name which translates to 'reward for good deeds', referencing the religious fasting that precedes this milkshake-like treat.[7]

In Lebanon and Syria as well as in Egypt, a cake made with semolina mixed with grated coconut, known variously as *hareeseh*, *harissa*, *hareesa*, *namoura* or *basbousa*, is served for Iftar and other Muslim celebrations. This dish is often prepared as small cakes covered with flavoured syrup; traditional recipes may include rose water or orange blossom water, flavours that reveal its Arab roots. A similar semolina and coconut cake is popular in Turkish, Greek, Armenian and Israeli cuisine. In an article in the *Jerusalem Post*, author Ruth Oliver remarks, 'It is almost impossible to celebrate Passover without coconut,' and she features recipes for coconut balls, coconut caramel flan and white chocolate squares with coconut.[8]

Coconut arrived on the east coast of Africa first through Arab and later through Portuguese traders. Vasco da Gama landed on the shores of Mozambique in 1498, and the Portuguese remained in the country for almost five hundred years until its independence in 1975. Unsurprisingly, cuisine in Mozambique bears significant Portuguese influence. Coconut crab curry, *caranguejo e coco*, is made with coconut milk and a spicy peri peri sauce (Swahili for 'pepper pepper'). Nando's, a South African restaurant chain with more than 1,000 branches in 35 countries, specializes in Portuguese food and was founded by Mozambique-born Fernando Duarte and South African-born Robert Brozin. The restaurant offers its own blend of peri peri sauce with coconut and lemon to 'create a uniquely Mozambican flavor'.[9]

Variations on coconut rice, made with coconut milk, are known throughout East Africa as *wali wa nazi* (Swahili for 'coconut rice') and are popular in the Indian Ocean port cities of Zanzibar, Lamu, Malindi and Mombasa. Many meat and seafood dishes and curries contain coconut milk, and coconut oil is the cooking oil of choice in the coastal regions.[10] Zanzibar is a virtual food hub, with a fusion of diverse influences from Arabia, Persia, Africa and India because of its position along the maritime trade routes. Restaurants here feature a traditional red curry with a coconut base.

As a general rule, serving dessert at the end of a meal is not common in Africa, and when a sweet is provided, it is often simply fresh fruit or a fruit salad. What desserts do appear tend to have been imported from Dutch, English and Portuguese cuisines. An exception is *kashata*, which is a coconut- and peanut-based sweet cookie baked on a hob, which is enjoyed in Kenya and throughout East Africa.

African coconut corn stew with a kanga, a woman's cloth wrapper with proverbs.

Dutch influence is evident in South African sweets. *Hertzoggie*, named for South African prime minister General J.B.M. Hertzog (1924 39), are mini jam and coconut tarts, often filled with apricot jam, and served for Muslim holidays. Author Gabeba Baderoon explains a 'coded history' of this sweet based on a dual political promise by Hertzog both to give women the vote and to establish equal rights for Muslims in the country. When he failed to accomplish this for the Malays, who were Muslim, the Malays baked and circulated the sweet with pink and chocolate icing and called it *twee-gevreetjie* or 'hypocrite'.[11]

Lamington cakes, originally from Australia, are small sponge cakes resembling a porcupine. They are dipped in chocolate and rolled in coconut. In South Africa, they are called *ystervarkies*, meaning 'porcupine' in Afrikaans.

Koesisters, a Cape Malay coconut-covered fried sweet popular in South Africa.

Coco de mer, Seychelles.

In Kenya, the government is training coconut nursery growers, hoping to boost economic development in coastal areas. The Coconut Development Authority is introducing early-maturing, high-yielding and disease-tolerant varieties. Similar initiatives are in progress in Mozambique, where coconut production has been extensively damaged by the years of civil war, as well as by rhinoceros beetle and lethal yellowing disease.

What tastes like coconut but has a slight citrusy flavour and is 'sexier'? Found only on the Seychelle Islands, off the coast of East Africa, coco de mer (*Lodoicea sechellarum*), known as sea coconut, double coconut or even, sometimes more graphically, the pubic coconut, is not actually a coconut palm

(*Cocos nucifera*) at all. The largest seed in the plant kingdom, coco de mer is a curiosity renowned for its unique shape, reminiscent of a woman's bottom and genitalia. With obvious fertility implications and touted as a powerful aphrodisiac, a coco de mer was presented as a gift to Prince William and his new wife Kate Middleton when they visited the Seychelles for their honeymoon in 2011. They needed a special licence from the government of the Seychelles to leave the country with the protected 'love nut'.

It is likely the British Royal couple never actually tasted coco de mer, but they may well have tried some of the many local dishes made with coconut that have Creole influence, including tarts, salad of palm hearts and palm wine. Served either hot or cold, *ladob* is a kind of stew that can be either sweet or savoury; it is made with coconut and plantains, bananas, cassava or breadfruit. Curries prepared with coconut milk include a national speciality, 'fruit-bat curry' made from megabat species indigenous to the Seychelles.[12]

Coconut is not indigenous to the Atlantic coast of Africa but was introduced there by Portuguese explorers, traders and missionaries in the 1500s. Names for the coconut in many indigenous languages translate as 'white man's nut'. The first coconut plantation in West Africa was established in Nigeria by Roman Catholic Missionaries in 1876. In recent years, as in other areas of the world, coconut palms in West Africa have been decimated by various diseases, including Cape St Paul wilt disease, which destroyed plantations and caused many processing companies to close. In September 2019 an international festival was held in Accra, Ghana, bringing together stakeholders in the coconut industry from all over the world to provide a platform to showcase the coconut and connect researchers, government agencies and industry leaders.

Coconut is often used in stew-like dishes in West Africa, especially along the coast, where it grows abundantly. There are numerous ideas from all over West Africa on how the iconic dish *mafe* or *maafe* should be prepared, including whether coconut should be an ingredient. *Mafe* originated in Mali in the 1800s, as European colonies were being established in West Africa, and became popular across the area, especially in Senegal and Gambia. The peanut is an essential ingredient in *mafe* and pairs well with coconut in this popular, hearty dish. Many adapted recipes call for commercial peanut butter rather than crushed peanut paste, and processed packaged

West African woman making *mafe*.

coconut, substitutions of which West African cooks would not approve.

In Nigeria, as well as Brazil and Sierra Leone, *frejon*, from the Portuguese word *feijao*, meaning 'beans', is a coconut bean soup traditionally served during Holy Week in Catholic Christian family celebrations. The dish is especially popular among Nigerian Yoruba who came back to Nigeria from Brazil after slavery was abolished there and settled in the Brazilian Quarters of Lagos. The beans are cooked slowly overnight and then blended with coconut milk to produce a thick, sweet pudding, often served with fish stew and peppered snails, appropriate for Good Friday, when dairy foods are forbidden. Nigerian Yoruba use coconut extensively in their religious practices, both in divination and as a preferred food offering on the altars to specific Orishas, or deities. Slaves brought these rituals to the New World, and coconut plays a part in contemporary Santeria ceremonies.

A treat in Angola, *cocada amarela*, 'yellow *cocadas*' (*cocadas* are coconut sweets), has its origins in Portuguese cuisine, which features many sweets made with egg yolks called *doces conventuais*. These sweets were invented by nuns in convents, where egg yolks were the by-product of the use of egg whites in the process of filtration of wine for communion and the production of starch for care of church vestments. *Cocada amarela*, flavoured with coconut, is popular in Mozambique and Cape Verde, as well as other former Portuguese colonies.[13]

In Senegal, Muslims celebrate Iftar, the breaking of the Ramadan fast, with a coconut rice pudding called *sombi*, which is similar to a creamy porridge. In North Africa, Moroccans enjoy drinking their chai with a coconut pudding called the *ghoriba*.

Traditional healers in Africa and the African diaspora recommend an infusion of boiling coconut root to aid digestion.

Extracts from coconut roots have been proven to be a reliable treatment for toothache and tooth-sensitivity, having anti-bacterial, antifungal, antiviral and antioxidant qualities.[14] In addition to its importance in traditional medicinal practices and culinary traditions, coconut has the potential to improve food security in parts of Africa.

Coconut palm illustration from Reverend Griffith Hughes's *Natural History of Barbados* (1750).

7
Europe and the Americas

Like many who regret not paying more attention in school, Columbus mournfully noted in his diary, 'There are trees of a thousand types, all with their various fruits and all scented. I am the saddest man in the world because I do not recognize them, for I am sure they are of great value in Spain for dyes and as medicinal spices.'[1]

On 17 November 1492 Christopher Columbus recorded in his journal that he had seen 'a large nut of the kind belonging to India', along with other spurious evidence supposedly proving he had indeed found his way to India and the Far East. He wrongly concluded that he was observing coconuts based on the description he had read of Marco Polo's encounters with this brown, round fruit. Experts now suggest Columbus actually came across a cacao, or chocolate, bean or the inedible small *nogal del país* (walnut). The trees he noted were more likely royal palms.[2]

The coconut made its way from the west coast of Africa as ballast and a convenient source of pure drinking water in slave-trading ships, continuing to this day to represent the New World and the romantic dream of the exotic 'other'. In the painting *William Penn Signing a Treaty with the Indians in Pennsylvania*, the painter Edward Savage depicts a palm, a tree

Edward Savage, *William Penn Signing a Treaty with the Indians in Pennsylvania*, *c.* 1800, oil on canvas.

which could not possibly have grown in this environment, but which vividly suggested new beginnings in the exotic New World. During the colonial period in the United States, coconuts arrived in the hold of trading ships passing through the West Indies to port cities all along the eastern and southern coasts of the country.

Both dried and fresh coconut were used in various recipes in colonial America. In *The Larder Invaded*, the authors describe colonial Philadelphia culinary history and note that street vendors regularly plied their wares, including coconut cakes from the West Indies, with rhyming calls.[3]

In South Carolina in 1770, Harriott Pinckney Horry, a member of a wealthy Charleston family, published a recipe for a confection named Coconut Puffs in *A Colonial Plantation Cookbook*.[4] This recipe is very similar to one found in the collection of recipes of her mother, Eliza Pinckney, who was born and raised in Antigua, in the West Indies, and was no doubt familiar with coconut. Sara Rutledge, known as Miss Sally, also lived in Charleston, and likely would have known of Harriott Pinckney Horry's cookbook. Miss Sally included a similar recipe for Cocoa-Nuts Puffs in her own book, *Carolina Housewife*, in 1847.

According to author Dave Dewitt, America's Founding Fathers were also 'Founding Foodies'; several of them, especially the Southerners, actually managed farms – on which much of their own food was grown – as 'gentlemen farmers'. Interested in new edibles, George Washington penned a letter on 22 July 1772, ordering culinary supplies for his estate, including coconut from Jamaica.[5]

While letters and records confirm that George Washington especially liked pineapple, it is highly likely that he encountered and enjoyed coconut as well. A trip to Barbados with his brother when he was a young man of nineteen is the only time the first American president ever left the United States. The coconut tree and its characteristics featured prominently in *The Natural History of Barbados* by Griffith Hughes, one of the books Washington is known to have studied before the trip and which he took with him. A number of sources report that one of Washington's favourite foods was mashed sweet potatoes with coconut, though evidence of this is not found in any original references, according to the Mount Vernon librarian Mary A. Thompson.[6] Famed lifestyle guru Martha Stewart offered an interesting update on colonial sweet potato recipes, using coconut milk in her Mashed Red-Curry Sweet Potatoes.[7]

Cooks throughout the United States are fond of preparing a chocolate-dipped coconut confection variously named Martha Washington coconut candy, bonbons or balls, though there is no historical record of Martha making this treat. Recipes often include Eagle Brand sweetened condensed milk, which was not developed by Gail Bordon until the early 1850s as a way to preserve milk safely. Condensed milk was especially useful as a military ration in the U.S. Civil War. A chain of sweet shops named 'Martha Washington Candies' was founded by Elie Sheetz in 1892, and at its height in the 1920s, it had hundreds of outlets all across the United States. Martha Washington candies were a featured confectionery in these shops, but only many years after it could possibly have been served as a dessert or treat for George by his wife Martha. In fact, Elie Sheetz trademarked the brand name 'Martha Washington Candies' in July 1906.

Thomas Jefferson kept a personal collection of recipes, including instructions for making puddings, with the suggestion that in addition to other ingredients, 'For a change . . . you may intermix with . . . dried coconut.'[8] Two versions of coconut pudding are included in author Marie Kimball's book *Thomas Jefferson's Cookbook*, a book that reproduces recipes in the Jefferson family that were handwritten by Virginia Randolph, Martha Jefferson Randolph's daughter.[9]

Many sources cite recipes for coconut macaroons as a preferred sweet of Thomas Jefferson. For example, macaroons are listed as one of Jefferson's favourites recipes in *Presidential Cookies* (2005) by Beverly Young. In fact, there *is* a handwritten recipe for 'macarons' in the Jefferson library collection, but there is no coconut in this ingredient list. Reflecting his appreciation of all things French, Jefferson's recipe, with its use of ground almonds, is essentially the same as that for a French macaron. This leads to the confusing discussion of macar*on*/ maca*roon*, coconut or almond? Culinary historians agree that both sweets have similar roots, but at some point, possibly in the early 1800s, in Italy, coconut was added or substituted for the ground almonds or almond paste. Jewish people in Italy liked this substitution, especially for Passover, a celebration

Passover coconut macaroons.

which forbids the use of leavening in food, and because the sweets made with shredded coconut did not spoil as quickly and were less easily damaged in shipping than the almond macaron. Though not mentioned in any religious materials, the product was developed for the Jewish holiday market in the 1800s. The coconut macaroon is so embedded in the Jewish tradition that it has become an almost essential element in the Passover celebration today.

Sharing culinary traditions is an important way to build a sense of community, whether for a religious ceremony like Passover, or for an everyday activity like drinking from a coconut shell water dipper. At the opposite extreme of the gold- and silver-embellished coconut cups collected during the Renaissance, which are prized in museum collections today, simple coconut dippers were found throughout colonial America. These dippers were ubiquitous in households as water receptacles prior to the invention of indoor plumbing. Coconut shell dippers, early disposables, were a commercial by-product of the processing of both the coconut flesh that would have been used in many popular nineteenth-century American desserts, and coir, the coconut husks used for rope and matting. Researcher Kathleen Kennedy describes examples of the sense of community evolving from personally sharing a coconut drinking vessel with others.[10] Thousands of these dippers were made and used. Similar wooden-handled coconut dippers are still popular in rural villages throughout Thailand and Laos today.

Edward Smith and E. Chapman Maltby were manufacturers of coconut-shell water dippers and other coconut products, including buttons and wooden spoons made from imported West Indies coconut in North Branford, Connecticut, in the 1870s. Their company had been discarding the coconut meat in the course of manufacturing, but when they developed a machine for easily separating coconut meat from its shell, they recognized new possibilities for coconut as a profitable food product. For a time, North Branford held the title 'Shredded Coconut Capital of the World'. In 1876 the inventors exhibited the machinery at the Philadelphia Centennial Exposition, winning first prize.

In 1892 Dunham Manufacturing Company of New York City and St Louis, Missouri, advertised their desiccated coconut, Dunham's Cocoanut, offering recipe books and game promotions requiring the collection of their package labels. A popular marketing promotion created for Dunham that is highly collectible today was a display shelf designed as a child's dolls' house, complete with a miniature kitchen stocked with Dunham coconut products. Franklin Baker, flour miller in

Philadelphia, has successfully sold grated coconut from the 1890s to this day and is a major brand in the United States.

Ships coming from the West Indies bringing coconut sailed to the southern U.S. ports of New Orleans, Charleston and Savannah. Many of the earliest documented recipes using coconut in the United States are from the nation's southern cooks, and coconut remains a popular ingredient in the regional cuisine today. Ambrosia, meaning 'food of the gods', is a worthy name for a dessert or salad that appeared first in the southern United States, where there was easy access to both oranges and coconut. The two ingredients were first documented in ambrosia recipes in cookbooks as early as the 1870s. Published by the Dunham Manufacturing Company in 1900, *60 Selected Cocoanut Receipts by Mary Tyson Rorer and Other Famous Cooks* contains instructions for making Heavenly Hash and Tropical Snow with similar ingredients and equally tempting names. Though coconut is the signature ingredient in ambrosia, variations abound. For example, bambrosinana is an over-the-top layered trifle-like dessert, alternating ambrosia with banana pudding and embellished with vanilla wafers, sliced bananas and maraschino cherries – and more coconut.[11]

Coconut pie and coconut cake are two of the most beloved coconut treats in the United States, and many families, particularly in the southern states, have cherished recipes that have been passed down for generations. Even the country's First Ladies have gotten in on the act. For example, First Lady Laura Bush has shared her Texas Buttermilk Coconut Pie with Whipped Cream, and Michelle Obama her crustless Coconut Pie.[12] 'Lady Bird' Johnson, wife of President Lyndon Johnson, has passed on a recipe for Lace Cookies that includes coconut.

In the collection of Emily Dickinson's (1830–1886) archived papers in the Poets House in New York City is a recipe

Bambrosinana coconut dessert.

for 'Cocoa Nut', or coconut, cake, in her own handwriting. Dickinson enjoyed baking and though the reclusive poet rarely left her home in Amherst, Massachusetts, she shared her baked treasures with children in the town by the unusual method of lowering a basket to them from her window. Dickinson researcher Vivian Pollak has calculated that more than 10 per cent of Dickinson's poems include images of food or drink, and Nelly Lambert suggests that perhaps a poem written on the back of a shared recipe 'describes blending exotic experiences with familiar ones – just as this cake blends tropical coconut with cream that likely came from a New England cow. Home mixes with adventure.'[13]

Alice B. Toklas and Gertrude Stein, expatriate Americans living in Paris from 1903 to 1946, were famously fond of cakes. Literary friend Natalie Barney described a get-together at which Alice served a 'fluffy confection of hers, probably a coconut layer cake which only Americans know how to make – and eat'.[14] A speciality of baking in the American South is the tall coconut layer cake, made possible after the invention of baking powder and baking soda. In her article titled 'Why Coconut Is the Star Ingredient of Southern Holiday', culinary writer Nancie McDermott gives credit for the first published coconut layer cake recipe to *The Blue Grass Cookbook*, published in 1904 by Minnie Fox and John Fox Jr.

There are several mentions of Lane cake, a tall, multi-layered cake with a bourbon and coconut filling, in Harper Lee's novel *To Kill a Mockingbird*. With lines such as, 'Miss Maudie Atkinson baked a Lane cake so loaded with shinny it made me tight,' the author uses food traditions to describe the setting of a small town in the South. 'Shinny' is a Southern slang word used for the liquor moonshine. The fluffy white icing is often also topped with shredded coconut. Especially popular during the Christmas holidays in the South, the cake is named after its originator, Emma Rylander Lane, of Clayton, Alabama, who first called it 'Prize Cake' in her self-published cookbook, *Some Good Things to Eat*, in 1898.[15]

Instructions for 'Bakers Easy Cut Up Party Cakes' are described in booklets and advertisements first published in 1956 and in print for more than thirty years. Coloured coconut garnishes transformed plain sheet cakes cut in various ways to form witches, bunnies and teddy bears for all occasions, and were particularly popular with children. Adults might prefer their sheet cakes prepared as 'poke' cakes, which are poked with holes for cream of coconut to saturate the baked cake and topped with shredded coconut.

A popular American cake is German chocolate cake, with its requisite coconut and pecan topping. The cake is not

'German' in any way but is the 1957 invention of Mrs George Clay, who used a type of baking chocolate developed by Samuel German for Baker's Chocolate company in 1852. General Foods, the parent company of Baker's, widely promoted this well-received 'recipe of the day', and sales of Baker's German's Sweet Chocolate skyrocketed.[16] The confusion about 'German' in the name of this cake embarrassed 'Lady Bird' Johnson when she served it to the German Chancellor Ludwig Erhard during a state dinner at President Johnson's ranch.[17]

Chocolate and coconut do make a particularly satisfying combination. Originally manufactured by the Peter Paul Candy Manufacturing Company, Almond Joy has been a popular American sweet since 1946; it consists of a coconut filling topped with almonds and covered in milk chocolate. The

Lane cake, based on a recipe by Edna Lewis.

Franklin Baker Witch cake.

Mounds bar, also by the Peter Paul Candy Manufacturing Company, debuted in 1920, and has coconut, with dark chocolate but no nuts. Both remain popular today. The successful advertising slogan 'Sometimes you feel like a nut, sometimes you don't' was conceived in 1970.

Similar to the Mounds bar, Bounty was introduced in the United Kingdom and Canada by the Mars Company in 1951. It offers a coconut filling covered with milk chocolate in a blue wrapper, and there is a dark chocolate version in a red wrapper. Both packages feature tropical beaches and coconut palms, advertising a taste of paradise. Mars sought to enter the American market with Bounty in 1989 but failed, even though in blind taste tests, Bounty was preferred. Americans are nostalgic about their childhood sweets.

Bounty chocolate coconut bar popular in the UK.

The British continue to enjoy their traditional coconut sweets such as coconut ice, a pink and white layered sweet, which is also popular in Australia and New Zealand. In Australia, this sweet is made with an ingredient called copha, known as 'white cloud', a form of vegetable shortening that is produced from hydrogenated coconut oil.[18] In the United States, a chocolate third layer is added to the sweet squares to make a treat known as a Neapolitan Coconut. The same sweet is popular in Mexico and marketed as Bandera de Coco, with white, red and green colouring added, in reference to the Mexican flag.

A local favourite in the Philadelphia area, available only seasonally around St Patrick's Day on 17 March, 'Irish Potatoes' are neither Irish nor potatoes but do contain coconut. In the early 1900s, Philadelphia was essentially the sweets capital of America, with more than two hundred manufacturers, as well as being one of the prime destinations for immigrants from Ireland. Coconut cream filling, often made with

Oh Ryan's Irish Potatoes.

A classic British sweet treat: coconut ice.

Philadelphia cream cheese and rolled in cinnamon, makes a treat resembling a miniature potato. Sales of these delights filled the lull between Valentine's Day and Easter sweets sales.

A more elegant coconut sweet is Raffaello, developed in 1990 by the Italian confectionery manufacturer Ferrero. Coconut covers a wafer sphere filled with sweet cream and an almond – definitely not something the home cook could easily make.

Coconut for flavouring and thickening of savoury food was introduced to British cooks during the colonial period through exposure to new foods while stationed throughout the British Empire, particularly in Sri Lanka and India. British cookbook writer Eliza Acton's *Modern Cookery* of 1845 contains seventeen coconut recipes, including savoury ones, with coconut used to thicken Indian curry and a savoury coconut soup. She also includes some coconut sweets with interesting names: the Printer's Pudding, made with breadcrumbs and coconut, and Bermuda Witches, very thin slices of sponge cake sandwiched with guava jelly and garnished with grated coconut and sprigs of myrtle.[19]

At about the same time, Amy Schauer (1871–1956) was writing cookbooks in Queensland, Australia, and included the popular Lamington cake, a Victoria sponge cake dipped in chocolate and rolled in coconut. The cake is so beloved that it has its own national day, 21 July. 'Lamington drives', in which the cakes are sold to raise funds for charities, are held on that day. While there are numerous theories, the most likely explanation for the Lamington name is Schauer's intent to honour Lady Lamington, the patroness of Brisbane Central Technical College, and not Lord Lamington, the Governor of Queensland (1896–1901), who referred to the cakes as 'bloody poofy wooly biscuits'.[20]

Back in London, the career of cookbook writer Eliza Acton was eclipsed by Mrs Beeton, whose name continues to be much better known from this period in the celebrity cookbook world. Mrs Beeton's 1907 edition of *Household Management: Guide to Cookery in All Branches* contained more than twenty recipes for coconut dishes, savoury and sweet, including the addition of coconut for thickening in a lobster and chicken curry, and a coconut soup very much like Acton's. Mrs Beeton's 1899 edition includes a helpful section entitled 'Provisions in India, General Observations on Indian Cookery', written for the English housewife who finds herself running a household in India.[21]

The process of producing desiccated coconut was developed in the 1880s. With this process, shipping a preserved form of coconut meat from Sri Lanka and India to Great Britain became practical. In the early 1900s, manufactured sweets were enjoying a booming market, and the preserved grated coconut and chocolate were prime ingredients.

While British cooks adopted coconut for sweets and curries, French and German recipes rarely included this ingredient. These countries were not as involved in the early establishment of coastal trade empires as Britain, Spain and Portugal. In a cuisine priding itself on using fresh, local ingredients, there is only one classic French recipe calling for coconut: a three-ingredient coconut macaron called *congolais*, referring to the former African colony of French Congo. In her cookbook, Alice B. Toklas goes so far as to say, 'For Parisians this classic fruit [coconut] from afar, amongst the pomegranates or oranges and pineapples, remains a useless curiosity.'[22]

Introduced by the Spanish during the colonial period, coconut palm grows freely along the coasts of Mexico, Central

America and South America. Many varieties of *cocadas*, coconut sweets, are widely enjoyed throughout the region, especially during the many festivals and religious holidays. Mexican artist Frida Kahlo was happiest when preparing food for elaborate fiestas, including family recipes for *cocadas* and coconut ice cream. Her recipe for coconut-stuffed candied limes is included in a cooking memoir, *Frida's Fiestas: Recipes and Reminiscences of Life with Frida Kahlo*, by her stepdaughter, Marie-Pierre Colle. Despite the joy cooking brought her, much of Kahlo's life was filled with pain, sadness and loneliness. In addition to the vivid images of her famous self-portraits, she was able to express these emotions in her still-life paintings of food. The arrangements of foods, their textures and colours, as well as their symbolism, were important themes in her paintings. The anthropomorphic form of coconuts was emphasized in her paintings *Weeping Coconuts* and *Coconut Tears*.

Frida Kahlo, *Weeping Coconuts*, 1951, oil on board.

Particularly in the Yucatán Peninsula of Mexico, many local families rely on selling street snacks based on coconut – an inexpensive, if not free, ingredient – for their primary or secondary incomes. These include *bolitas de coco* (coconut balls), *coco paletas* (coconut ice lollies), *pays de coco* (coconut pies) and *cocos fríos* (cold coconut water).

The range of uses and the variety of values placed on coconut in that part of the world today are readily apparent in a small one-block area in the Colombian port city of Cartagena. Street vendors coming in from the outskirts of the city offer fresh green coconuts to drink from with straws at the equivalent cost of only a dollar or two in U.S. currency, while supermarkets sell them for twice the price. In a newly opened lifestyle shop, these same coconuts are polished to gleaming and sold as purely ornamental in a pretty bowl for $9 each, serving no practical function at all. On the street, locals cut the shells into bowls, polishing them and selling them for as little as $1. In this same city block, exclusive, high-end restaurants offer innovative chef's presentations of coconut, such as *ceviche en coco*, raw fish marinated in citrus and served with coconut, for $25 a portion. Even more expensive is *langosta isleña*, lobster finished with coconut milk and white and black coconut rice, while nearby on the street, traditional simpler dishes of chicken and fresh fish cooked in coconut milk sell for $5. In the historic district of Cartagena, there is a particular street arcade called the Portal de Los Dulces (hall of sweets), where the finest home-made, traditional-recipe *cocadas* made by true experts are on offer daily. The main ingredients are grated coconut, cinnamon, sugar, coconut water and milk, along with a variety of flavourings, including guava and pineapple. A popular and unique choice of sweet at the Portal is a doll-shaped sweet, *muñecas de leche*, literally 'milk dolls'.[23]

Ceviche en coco, from Candé restaurant in Cartagena, Colombia.

In Argentina, the *alfajor*, a sandwich cookie or wagon-wheel-type baked good filled with dulce de leche (thick caramel sauce) and rolled in shredded coconut, is considered the national biscuit and is a staple in every bakery there. The treat originated in Spain, where it is a traditional Christmas confection; the coconut is a New World embellishment.

Brazilians share the regional sweet tooth and love of *cocadas*. Popular *beijinhos de coco*, or 'little kisses' in Portuguese, are also known as *branquinho*, or 'little white ones'. Other sweets made with coconut include Brazilian coconut cakes (*bom-bocado de coco*), coconut pudding (*manjar de coco*) and an unusual combination of coconut and Parmesan cheese (*queijadinha*), which is shared while lingering around the table after a meal, a practice called *sobremesa*.[24]

Brazilian cuisine features savouries as well as sweets made from coconut. *Moqueca* is a fish stew made with firm white fish, onions, garlic, bell peppers, tomatoes, coriander and coconut milk that takes different forms throughout the country. Ingredients for this popular dish vary widely throughout Brazil. For example, in northeast coastal Brazil, the regional cuisine of Bahia is influenced by African foodways, including the common use of coconut. *Vatapá* is a shrimp stew requiring both coconut milk and palm oil, thickened into a paste

Stall of *cocadas* in Cartagena, Colombia.

with bread or manioc or cassava flour, which can include ground peanuts or cashews, onions, tomatoes, ginger, okra and chillies.

Culinary researchers are only beginning to recognize the important contribution of African influences on the food traditions of the diaspora. *Callaloo* and crab represent a national dish and staple for Trinidadians, and has roots in so-called 'slave food'. In Africa, *callaloo*, stewed greens, would have been prepared using palm oil, not widely available in the Caribbean, but slaves in the 1530s used coconut oil.[25]

Jamaican cuisine features coconut as an important ingredient. A local favourite, sweet potato pudding, is made with spices, sweet potatoes, coconut milk and dried fruits and has been described as 'Like a slice of all things Jamaica on a plate'. An even more colourful saying, 'hell a top, hell a bottom and hallelujah in the middle', refers to how the pudding is traditionally cooked on a coal stove, with the pot of pudding in its pan on the coals and a zinc plate on top of it with more coals. The pudding takes up to five hours to bake, and the fire has to be constantly tended.[26]

Grizzada is a coconut pastry with Portuguese heritage; it is a small round tart with grated coconut popular in Jamaica. Jamaican coco bread, made with flour and yeast with coconut milk, firm on the outside and tender on the inside with buttery layers, is used for all kinds of sandwiches. Simple daily rice and peas are cooked with coconut milk in Jamaica. *Bammy*, also popular in both Belize and Costa Rica, consists of grated cassava shaped into discs soaked in coconut milk and then fried. This starch is thought to have been a part of the native Arawak diet from pre-Columbian times. Run down (run dun) is a fish stew slow-cooked in coconut milk, whose name comes from a technique of slow-cooking until the fish has completely fallen apart. It is often made with mackerel, which is considered a poor man's fish.[27] More recently developed for tourists, a popular cocktail with roots in Jamaica's local ingredients is the Dirty Banana – rum cream, Tia Maria, coconut cream, fresh banana, ice cream, coffee liquor and/or chocolate syrup.

There are street vendors on many corners selling fresh coconut drinks in Havana, Cuba, today. *Saoco* is a drink with roots going back into the era of slavery, and the cheap combination of *aguardiente* (a sugar-cane-based spirit), coconut water, lime and sugar or honey is thought to have been used as a medicinal tonic. The beverage is now made with rum. Coconut, along with brown sugar, is a familiar component of popular desserts, including bread pudding, rice pudding and custards.[28]

Coconut is a popular element of Puerto Rican cuisine, especially during Christmas holidays. Seasonal delicacies include *arroz con dulce*, rice cooked with coconut milk, flavoured with sugar, cinnamon, nutmeg and cloves and garnished with cinnamon sticks and raisins. Another favourite, *tembleque*, is a smoother creamy coconut pudding. *Coquito* is a milky coconut drink similar to eggnog, made with cream of coconut, coconut milk, sweetened condensed milk, rum and vanilla and served with a cinnamon stick for Christmas.[29] An everyday favourite, Coco Rico is the cola drink of Puerto Rico, a ubiquitous carbonated coconut beverage with a light flavour similar to 7Up or a British lemonade.

Conkies are a traditional Barbadian dessert or snack especially popular during the island's Independence Day celebrations in November. Ingredients include pumpkin, cornmeal, sweet potatoes and coconut, flavoured with local spices and raisins and cooked in banana leaves. A similar sweet is known as *paime* in Saint Lucia and the islands of Trinidad and

Tobago. The treat is also now a part of Creole Day celebrations held in Saint Lucia on the last Sunday of October.

The Guna, an indigenous people of Panama and Colombia, live on autonomous reservations on the San Blas Islands of Panama and in a few small villages on the mainland. Harvesting and trading coconuts, which are plentiful on all the islands, and more recently, income from limited tourism, are their means of survival. Guna proudly serve their traditional red snapper with coconut rice and the *coco loco*, a fresh coconut filled with some rum. Coconut is an important form of currency in this simple culture, and it is illegal to take a coconut off the islands.[30]

8

The Future of Coconut

In the 1950s coconut producers such as Franklin Baker and Dunham marketed their products extensively to housewives. They stressed the exotic nature of coconut and its easy application in baking cakes and pies and in ambrosia, as well as in other dishes. While the coconut cut-up cakes of the 1950s may have fallen out of vogue, new uses for a variety of coconut products, including growing interest in Thai and Indian foods, have filled that gap, creating new culinary opportunities. There is good reason to believe those opportunities will increase.

According to a February 2020 Research and Markets report, the global coconut market is expected to grow at a CAGR (compound annual growth rate) of 13.5 per cent during the forecast period of 2019–26.[1] However, ageing coconut trees and lack of economic incentive for growers to plant new ones may prevent coconut products from reaching their full economic potential. There are promising future large markets for coconut oil in the plant-based meats industry that is expanding as demand for vegan and vegetarian alternatives continues to climb, with the products becoming both popular and profitable. Another potential market is for coconut water as a soft drink substitute. If these and other opportunities are to be fully realized, there needs to be more dependable sources for coconut and consistently better quality control.

Human activities have contributed to the decline in quantity and quality of coconut trees, with older trees not being replaced and entire plantations being cut down for development. In many cases, farmers will need economic incentives to overcome these issues, and there is a strong role for government agencies to help with the introduction and facilitation of new technology to improve productivity. This includes financial and technical assistance in relation to the proper use of insecticides, intercropping, soil enhancement and harvesting. Government development agencies in coconut-growing areas have also been working on developing mechanical harvesters and training farmers on safe tree-climbing methods. Research facilities can also explore improved varieties that have higher productivity and are easier to harvest.

Natural hazards such as hurricanes have decimated some coconut-growing areas. Lethal yellowing disease and pests such as coconut mites have also taken their toll. Preserving and developing varieties that can better withstand natural hazards or that have particular disease-resistance qualities will be critical in order to increase coconut production and make coconut farming more profitable. In order to preserve the coconut genetic resources, researchers are developing germ banks and pollen cryopreservation.[2] The International Coconut Genebank for Latin America and the Caribbean is engaged in conservation activities to identify disease-resistant genes, particularly against lethal yellowing.

Researchers are actively developing and promoting varieties of coconuts which have qualities important for specific uses. For example, scientists have determined the gene responsible for giving the Thai aromatic coconut its pandan-like aroma, and this allows researchers to produce new varieties of coconut with pleasing aromas and tastes.[3] The government of the Philippines has been actively promoting the cultivation and promotion of *macapuno*, a uniquely Filipino product.

The coconut palm is a symbol of the city of Salalah, Oman, where there is considerable interest in developing value-added uses of the coconut fruit, from beverages and edibles, to fertilizer. Oman's Ministry of Agriculture and Fisheries, through its Model Farm for Coconut Trees and Product Manufacturing Program, is presently expending considerable resources to encourage the establishment of additional coconut plantations with modern irrigation systems and more advanced horticultural practices.

In 2018 the Government Export Promotion Authority (GEPA) of Ghana launched its Coconut Export Revitalization

Thai coconut-flavoured M&MS with signature pandan aroma.

Horticultural practice of intercropping banana and coconut, a government initiative in Oman.

Project, describing coconut as 'a cash crop with a high potential of boosting the economy and creating jobs'.[4] It has provided seedlings for new varieties of coconut, and technology resources to encourage new farmers and support existing smallholder farmers. Strengthening the coconut supply chain will help increase revenues paid to farmers for their coconuts.

A concern for all farmers, especially coconut farmers, is that commodity prices can fluctuate wildly. Government efforts to stabilize prices help to address this, along with encouraging farmers to interplant coconut trees with other crops. This supports the farmer in years in which prices for coconuts are low, or during the growth period when new coconut plants have not yet come into production.

The use of pesticides results in higher coconut production and the preservation of trees that may otherwise suffer from pests. But the farmer must consider that he may obtain a higher price for untreated coconut. Only untreated coconut is considered organic, and there is a growing market for organic coconut oil. Conversely, economic analysis of coconuts treated with abamectin to combat the coconut mite, compared to untreated coconuts, shows that, regardless of the market destination, the resulting higher productivity significantly offsets the cost of the pesticide treatment, resulting in a 69 per cent higher profit using the pesticide.[5]

Finding ways to utilize the waste from coconut processing can enhance overall profitability. Encouraging developing countries to design and produce value-added products can also boost coconut economics. For example, *nata de coco*, produced by the fermentation of coconut water, a simple product traditionally made in homes in the Philippines, found a new market as a popular fad diet food in Japan.

Building on the idea of terroir and artisanal speciality food products, France's Institut Oenologique de Champagne has collaborated with the Philippines to produce an artisanal coconut wine (*kahal*) called Royal Chief Coconut Wine. This wine is produced from the water of young coconuts and the taste of the water reflects the terroir, which refers to the characteristic taste and flavour imparted to a wine by the environment – including the soil and the climate – in which it is produced.

Resolution of the confusing 'bad for you' fats question and dissemination of correct nutritional information will ease health-conscious consumers' concerns about coconut oil. It will also be important in the marketing of new coconut products, particularly those products using coconut oil. A more nuanced explanation of health risks and the advantages of coconut oil is that although it is a saturated fat, it is a type of saturated fat, lauric acid, known to be 'healthy'.[6]

There is considerable market potential for promoting coconut water as a healthier substitute for soft drinks containing high-fructose corn syrup. Although there are concerns about producers diluting coconut water with sugar water, newly developed methods to detect adulteration should reduce the practice and improve consumer confidence in the purity of the product.[7] Progress has also been made in improving the flavour retention qualities of pasteurized coconut water. Franklin Baker ships a frozen concentrate from the Philippines to be reconstituted by processors in the United States, resulting in coconut water at a more reasonable price. Blending coconut water with other products such as grape juice provides a new use for both coconut water and fruit juices.

Selling whole young coconuts for coconut water has quite a few challenges. The coconut needs to be fresh to be tasty, and the flavour of coconut water depends on the age of the coconut and where it is grown. One Vietnamese company, Hamona, has included the date picked and a location identifier for each coconut in its marketing, so individuals can choose

Bullet coffee with a shot of coconut oil in Bali, Indonesia, alongside a cocolele, a Filipino ukulele made from coconut.

Coconuts with flip tops, sold in a Waitrose supermarket in London.

the exact type they want. These coconuts are tagged with a unique code that the consumer can enter on Hamona's website to learn exactly from which tree their particular coconut was harvested, at what farm the tree is located and by whom the farm is owned, and find out the story of that particular farmer. Purchasers are also invited to rate the quality of their coconut drinks. The website provides virtually hundreds of recipes, from savouries to sweets, and instructs users on how to open the coconut and eat it.[8] Other innovative suppliers have marketed young coconuts fitted with flip-top openings for a straw, making them easier to drink.

Fermented coconut products have a potential niche in the health food arena. The fermented drinks kombucha and kefir can be made from coconut water and coconut milk, respectively. *Nata de coco* is made from fermented coconut water and has a more jelly-like consistency. Coconut soy sauce made from coconut water is also available. These products fill a market niche for fermented products while offering a soy-free option for those allergic to soybeans.

Coconut protein powder has applications as an emulsifier, and with 33 per cent protein, provides an additional benefit to enhance processed foods.[9] Gluten free and high in fibre, coconut flour also has marketing potential, and can be added to energy bars. However, its domestic use is limited because of the difficulty in getting the right texture. For

Coconut flavouring is used in unexpected food products, such as this coconut Gouda cheese.

example, if coconut flour is substituted on a 1:1 basis it will adversely affect the texture of the intended products, making them more dense. Frequently, a portion of the flour in the recipe is substituted with coconut flour, with wheat flour used for the remainder. While this strategy may be used to get the proper texture, adding any wheat flour prevents the product from being labelled as gluten free.

Likewise, coconut sugar does not behave like cane sugar in baked goods. A first step in most biscuit or dessert pie recipes is to cream together the butter and sugar, but coconut sugar doesn't cream in a similar manner. So while health food consumers may prefer coconut sugar, with its lower glycaemic index, the home cook may have more difficulty incorporating coconut sugar into typical recipes.

Plant-based meatless burgers frequently contain coconut oil, which should theoretically place this product in the healthy food category. However, these burgers also contain chemicals as flavour enhancers and preservatives, which may alienate those who are health-food friendly. Plus, researchers at Kansas State University speculate that the 'environmental foot print' of a meatless burger made with coconut oil is worse than a beef burger because the coconut oil usually must be imported from a distance, and the impact of transport on the environment negates the advantage of a meatless burger.[10]

There are existential questions about the future of the coconut: how can the coconut be developed in a non-exploitative way that does not repeat the mistakes of the past? Will we ensure that coconut growing and processing will be sustainable, both in environmental terms and in terms of human costs? Will we protect small landholder farmers trying to produce coconut oil? We would do well to be mindful of the old Filipino saying, 'He who grinds the poor will only grind water instead of oil from the coconut.'[11]

Perhaps a more encouraging proverb comes from the Pacific Islands: 'He who plants a coconut tree plants food and drink vessels and clothing, a habitation for himself and a heritage for his children.'[12]

Recipes

Coconut Dinner Menu

We invite you to create your own memorable coconut-themed menu with suggestions below for each course. You might want to tie in your menu with a special occasion, holiday or celebration by breaking a coconut to start a new adventure. Or perhaps plan a celebration of World Coconut Day on 2 September.

Cocktails and Drinks

piña colada (Puerto Rico)
any tiki drink, and don't forget the paper umbrellas (Hawaii)
coconut wine (for example, *lambanog* or *kabal* from the Philippines)
limonada, a lemonade made with coconut water (Colombia)
coconut water
health food drink: ginger, turmeric and coconut oil

Starters

coconut fried shrimp
serabi, *khanom khrok* (coconut and rice flour street food in Indonesia and Thailand)

spiced onion fritters with coconut chutney (India)
lumpia (spring rolls) made with *ubod* (heart of coconut palm) (Philippines)
pumpkin flower stuffed with *latik*, or coconut curd (Philippines)

Mains

adobo (Philippines)
beef *rendang* (Indonesia)
curry with coconut milk (India)
mafi (African chicken stew with coconut milk)
moqueca (fish stew with coconut milk) (Brazil)

Side Dishes

coconut rice (lots of variations from Caribbean to Indonesian *thengai sadam*)
coconut braised collard greens (West Africa and the Caribbean)
kale *mallum* (greens cooked in coconut milk) (Sri Lanka)
coconut chicken soup (Thailand)
red lentil soup with coconut milk (India, Thailand)
callaloo (Caribbean)
coconut chutney (India)
sambol (Indonesia, Malaysia)
ginataang gulay (vegetables in coconut milk) (Philippines)
pani popo (Samoan coconut bread)

Desserts

ambrosia (fruit salad with coconut) (U.S.)
'Nine Auspicious Thai desserts'
barfi (a fudge-like sweet made with coconut milk) (India)
macapuno coconut ice cream (Philippines)

Vietnamese wedding cakes in banana leaves
various coconut cakes from around the world with coconut in the cake and/or the topping: Lane cake (USA), Lamington cake (Australia), Toto (Jamaica) or Queen Elizabeth Cake (UK)
coconut macaroons
Irish potato sweets
candied coconut (Vietnam)
mango sticky rice with coconut cream sauce (Thailand)
sombi (African coconut pudding)
ube-macapuno cake (Philippines)

Recipes

Cocoa Nut Puffs

From *A Colonial Plantation Cookbook: The Receipt Book of Harriott Pinckney Horry, 1770*

Take a Cocoa Nut and dry it well before the fire, then grate it and add to it a good spoonful of Butter, sugar to your taste, six Eggs with half the whites and 2 spoonfulls of rose water. Mix them all together and they must be well beat before they are put in the Oven.

Cocoa-nut Cream

From Mary Randolph, *The Virginia Housewife* (1824)

Take the nut from its shell, pare it and grate it very fine; mix it with a quart [0.95 l] of cream, sweeten and freeze it. If the nut be a small one, it will require one and a half to flavour a quart of cream.

Cocoa-nut Pudding

From Eliza Leslie, *Seventy-five Receipts for Pastry, Cakes and Sweetmeats* (1828)

a quarter of a pound [115 g] of cocoa-nut, grated
a quarter of a pound [115 g] of powdered white sugar
three ounces and a half [100 g] of fresh butter
the whites only of six eggs
half a glass of wine and brandy mixed
half a tea-spoonful of rose-water

Break up a cocoa-nut, and take the thin brown skin carefully off, with a knife. Wash all the pieces in cold water, and then wipe them dry, with a clean towel. Weigh a quarter of a pound of cocoa-nut, and grate it very fine, into a soup-plate.

Stir the butter and sugar to a cream, and add the liquor and rose-water gradually to them.

Beat the whites only, of six eggs, till they stand alone on the rods; and then stir the beaten white of egg, gradually, into the butter and sugar. Afterwards, sprinkle in, by degrees, the grated cocoa-nut, stirring hard all the time. Then stir all very well at the last.

Have ready a puff-paste, sufficient to cover the bottom, sides and edges of a soup-plate. Put in the mixture, and bake it in a moderate oven, about half an hour.

Grate loaf-sugar over it, when cool.

Mrs Beeton's Coconut Soup, *Potage au Noix de Coco*

From *Mrs Beeton's Book of Household Management* (1861)

Ingredients – 2 quarts [1.9 l] of second stock [Second stock is the second boiling of meat bones sometimes called ordinary or household stock], 4 ozs. [115 G] of grated coconut, preferably fresh, 2 ozs. [60 g] of rice flour, 2 Tablespoons of cream, mace, salt and pepper.

Method – When desiccated coconut is used it should be previously soaked for 2 or 3 hours in a little of the stock. Boil the stock, add a small blade of mace and the coconut, and simmer gently for 1 hour. Mix the rice flour smoothly with a little stock, boil the remainder, add the blended rice flour and stir and boil gently for about 10 minutes. Season to taste, stir in the cream and serve.

Mrs Tyson's Coconut Macaroon

From *Sixty Selected Cocoanut Receipts by Mrs. Sarah Tyson Rorer and Other Famous Cooks* (1900)

Beat the whites of five eggs to a stiff froth; fold in carefully a half pound of powdered sugar [230 g], sifted, a cup and a half [140 g] of Dunham's Cocoanut [desiccated coconut]; stir very lightly and drop by spoonfuls on oiled paper, and bake in a slow oven twenty minutes. When done take out, and when cool moisten the under side of the paper, and the macaroons may be easily loosened.

In the nineteenth century, the list of ingredients in cookbooks shows the influence of national and commercial brands, mass produced food and global influences. Examples include Baker's Coconut and Dunham's Cocoanut.

Dunham Coconut Surprise

From Dunham *Good Housekeeping* advertisement in 1903

Chop one package Dunham's Coconut and soften with a little boiling water, add 4 teaspoonsful powered sugar. Spread thickly on slices of bread or sponge cake. Add another layer and pyramid of Jelly.

Mrs Watson's Toasted Coconut Cream Pie

Adapted from www.chowhound.com, 'Tavern Restaurant Coconut Cream pie'

1 envelope gelatine (1/4 oz, 7 g)
80 ml (1/3 cup) cold milk
3 eggs, separated
60 g (1/2 cup) sugar
160 ml (2/3 cup) milk
pinch of salt
240 ml (1 cup) whipping cream
2 tsp vanilla
1 25 cm (10 in.) pie shell, baked and cooled
100 g (1 1/3 cups) coconut, toasted

Dissolve gelatine in 80 ml (1/3 cup) cold milk. Let stand. Separate eggs; to yolks, add 60 g (1/2 cup) sugar and beat together. Scald 160 ml (2/3 cup) milk; add egg and sugar mixture to milk. Cook until thickened. Remove from stove and add gelatine. Put in refrigerator until set, about half-hour. Beat egg whites with a pinch of salt. Fold egg whites into mixture. Whip cream and add vanilla. Fold into mixture. Fill the pie shell. Toast the coconut until golden, cool and sprinkle on pie. Refrigerate pie for a few hours.

Michelle Obama's Crustless Coconut Pie

Adapted from 'Obama Family Recipes to Meet Inauguration Day in Good Taste' by Bill Kennedy, The Plain Dealer, www.cleveland.com, accessed 2 November 2019

60 g (1/4 cup) butter
190 g (1 1/2 cups) sugar
3 eggs
240 ml (1 cup) milk
60 g (1/2 cup) flour
100 g (1 1/3 cups) flaked coconut
1 tsp vanilla

½ tsp freshly grated nutmeg
optional: whipped cream, thin slices of lime or lemon, or sprig of mint for garnish

Cream butter and sugar then add eggs one at a time. Add milk and flour until blended. Stir in coconut, nutmeg and vanilla. Pour into pie pan and bake at 180°C (350°F) for 45 minutes.

Edna Lewis's Famous Coconut Lane Cake

The Edna Lewis Cookbook (1972), adapted from www.oprah.com, accessed 12 April 2021

Cake

230 g (1 cup) butter, room temperature, plus extra for pans
435 g (3½ cups) cake flour, plus extra for pans
1 tbsp baking powder
¼ tsp salt
240 ml (1 cup) milk, room temperature
1 tsp vanilla extract
380 g (2 cups) sugar
8 large egg whites, room temperature

Icing

12 large egg yolks
225 g (1½ cups) sugar
170 g (¾ cup) unsalted butter, melted
150 g (1½ cups) finely chopped pecans
240 g (1½ cups) finely chopped raisins
115 g (1½ cups) unsweetened coconut flakes
1½ tsp vanilla extract
120 ml (½ cup) bourbon

Cake: preheat oven to 160°C (325°F). Butter and flour three 23 cm (9 in.) cake pans. In a bowl, sift together flour, baking powder and salt; set aside. In another small bowl, mix together milk and vanilla and set aside.

Cream butter and sugar until light and fluffy. Add the flour and milk mixtures in 2 or 3 batches, beginning and ending with flour.

In a separate bowl, beat egg whites until soft peaks form. Stir ⅓ of egg whites into the batter. Gently fold in the remaining egg whites. Pour batter into the prepared pans and bake 20 to 25 minutes. Remove from oven and let cool on wire racks 10 minutes. Loosen sides with a knife and invert cakes onto racks; cool completely before icing.

Icing: in a medium saucepan over medium heat, whisk egg yolks and sugar together until sugar dissolves. Stirring constantly, add melted butter until thick enough to coat the back of a spoon, 1 to 3 minutes. Do not let the mixture simmer or boil. Add pecans, raisins and coconut; cook 1 minute. Remove from heat; add the vanilla and bourbon. Cool to room temperature before using. Spread 240 g (¾ cup) icing between each layer of cake; use the rest for the sides and top.

Hindu Coconut Soup

Adapted from *The Land* (Sydney, NSW, 15 September 1922); repr. at 'A Coconut Menu', www.theoldfoodie.com, accessed 10 May 2021

Add the grated meat of half a fresh coconut to 0.95 l (1 quart) of white stock. Cook slowly for 20 minutes, and then strain through cheesecloth. Add the juice of a lemon and season to taste. Pour the mixture on the beaten yolks of 2 eggs, heat in a double broiler until thickened, and serve boiled rice with the soup.

Coconut Flour Brownies

Adapted from Bruce Fife, *Cooking with Coconut Flour* (Colorado Springs, CO, 2005)

75 g (⅓ cup) coconut oil
40 g (½ cup) cocoa powder
6 eggs

190 g (1 cup) sugar
½ tsp salt
½ tsp vanilla
60 g (½ cup) sifted coconut flour
100 g (1 cup) nuts, chopped (optional)

Blend coconut oil and cocoa powder together in a saucepan on low heat. Remove from heat and let cool. Mix together eggs, sugar, salt and vanilla in a separate bowl. Stir in cocoa cooled mixture. Add coconut flour and stir until there are no lumps. Add nuts. Pour batter into a greased 8 x 20 × 20 × 5 cm (8 × 2 in.) pan. Bake at 120°C (250°F) for 30–35 minutes.

Fresh Coconut *Sambol*

From authors' cooking school experiences in Sri Lanka, Bali, the Philippines and India

1 tsp chopped dried red finger-length chilli
1 tbsp finely chopped onion
1 tsp pepper
1 tsp dried Maldive fish powder, a cured dried tuna fish frequently used in Sri Lanka (alternatively use the same amount of ground dried prawns or fish sauce)
200 g (2 cups) freshly grated coconut
3 tbsp lime or lemon juice
salt to taste

In a blender, grind until smooth the chilli, onion, pepper and Maldive fish powder, dried prawns, or fish sauce. Add the coconut. Season with the lime or lemon juice and salt. Mix well by hand.

References

Introduction

1 Jennifer Epstein, 'On a Beach', www.politico.com, 10 June 2014.

2 Diana Lutz, 'Deep History of Coconuts Decoded', https://source.wustl.edu, 24 June 2011.

3 Kenneth P. Emory, 'Every Man His Own Robinson Crusoe', *National History Magazine* (June 1943).

4 Kat Eschner, 'Why JFK Kept a Coconut Shell in the Oval Office', www.smithsonianmag.com, 2 August 2017.

5 Charles Darwin, *The Foundation of the Origin of Species: Two Essays Written in 1842 and 1844*, ed. Francis Darwin (Cambridge, 1909), facs. available at http://darwin-online.org.uk, accessed 7 November 2019.

6 Harold Hamel Smith and Fred Pape, 'Foreword', in *Coco-nuts: The Consols of the East* (Charleston, SC, 2010), p. xvi.

1 From Roots to Fruit: Botany, Production and Health

1 Fred Gray, *Palm* (London, 2018), p. 68.

2 Alastair Bland, 'The Tallest, Strongest and Most Iconic Trees in the World', www.smithsonian.com, 5 July 2012.

3 Annie Deeter, *The Coconut Bible: The Complete Coconut Reference Guide* (London, 2015), p. 60.

4 Mike Foale and Hugh Harries, 'Farm and Forestry Production and Marketing Profile for Coconut (*Cocos nucifera*)', in *Specialty Crops for Pacific Island Agroforestry: Permanent Agriculture Resources*, ed. C. R. Elevitch (Holualoa, HI, 2011), p. 6.

5 S. C. Ahuja et al., 'Coconut: History, Uses, and Folklore', *Asian Agri-history*, XVIII/3 (2014), pp. 221–48.

6 Abayomi Jegede, 'Top 10 Largest Coconut Producing Countries in the World', www.thedailyrecords.com, 1 January 2019.

7 Ibid.

8 Food and Agriculture Organization of the United Nations (FAO), 'Coconut Information Sheet', www.fao.org, January 2001.

9 Bland, 'The Tallest'.

10 Foale and Harries, 'Farm and Forestry Production and Marketing Profile for Coconut (*Cocos nucifera*)', pp. 13–15.

11 Hubert Omont, 'Information Sheet, Coconut', www.agris.fao.org, accessed 20 November 2019.

12 Winner, 'Economic Potential Unlocked in Coconut', www.winner-tips.org, accessed 20 November 2019.

13 Cited in Justin William Moyer, 'The Murky Ethics of Making Monkeys Pick Our Coconuts', *Washington Post* (10 October 2015).

14 E. W. Gudger, 'Monkeys Trained as Harvesters', *Natural History,* www.naturalhistorymag.com, accessed 21 November 2019.

15 See Christian Kracht, *Imperium: A Fiction of the South Seas* (New York, 2016).

16 Jan Dodd, *The Rough Guide to Vietnam* (London, 2003), p. 142.

17 Ahuja et al., 'Coconut: History, Uses, and Folklore', p. 233.

18 E. B. Lima et al., '*Cocos nucifera* (L.) (Arecaceae): A Phytochemical and Pharmacological Review', *Brazilian*

Journal of Medical and Biological Research, XI/11 (August 2015), pp. 953–64.

19 Ashley Mays, 'Coconut Oil Isn't Healthy. It's Never Been Healthy', USA *Today* (21 June 2017); J. J. Virgin, 'Yes, Coconut Oil Is Still Healthy. It's Always Been Healthy', www.huffpost.com, 26 June 2017.

20 Deeter, *The Coconut Bible*, p. 118.

21 'Coconut Oil', The Nutrition Source, Harvard School of Public Health, www.hsph.harvard.edu, accessed 14 June 2020.

22 Ahuja et al., 'Coconut: History, Uses, and Folklore', p. 228.

2 A Long and Fabled Story

1 Raden S. Roosman, 'Coconut, Breadfruit and Taro in Pacific Oral Literature', *Journal of the Polynesian Society*, LXXIX/2 (June 1970), pp. 219–32.

2 N. M. Nayer, *The Coconut: Phylogeny, Origins and Spread* (Cambridge, MA, 2017), p. 56.

3 B. F. Gunn et al., *'Independent Origins of Cultivated Coconut (Cocos nucifera L.)* in the Old World Tropics ', *Plos One* (22 June 2011), p. 1.

4 Nayer, *The Coconut*, p. 14.

5 H. C. Harries and C. R. Clement, 'Long-distance Dispersal of the Coconut Palm by Migration within the Coral Atoll Ecosystem', *Annals of Botany*, CXIII/4 (March 2014), pp. 565–70.

6 Rachel Laudan, *Cuisine and Empire: Cooking in World History* (Berkeley, CA, 2015), p. 20.

7 *The Tales of Sinbad, The Fifth Voyage of Sinbad the Seaman*, 17th–18th century, https://middleeast.library.cornel.edu, accessed 15 April 2021.

8 See Thomas Wright, ed., *The Travels of Marco Polo* (London, 1854).

9 Tim Mackintosh-Smith, ed., *The Travels of Ibn Battutah by Ibn Battutah* (New York, 2016).

10 Charles Clement, 'Coconuts in the Americas', *Botanical Review*, LXXIX (2013), pp. 342–70.

11 Jonathan D. Sauer, *Historical Geography of Crop Plants: A Select Roster* (New York, 1993), p. 188.

12 Jonathan Jones, 'James Cook: The Voyages Review: Eye-opening Records of Colliding Worlds', www.theguardian.com, 26 April 2018.

13 Annie Deeter, *The Coconut Bible: The Complete Coconut Reference Guide* (London, 2015), p. 26.

14 Ibid.

15 David Leeming, *The Oxford Companion to World Mythology* (Oxford, 2005), p. 201.

16 Ibid., p. 181.

17 'Coconut and Soap: Is There a Connection?', *Fish Friers Review* (October 1988), p. 22.

18 'Best Type of Oil for Deep Frying Fish', www.webstaurantstore.com, accessed 21 November 2019.

19 'Glycerin Soap and Glycerin', www.chagrinvalleysoapandsalve.com, 29 July 2014.

20 Jagath C. Savandasa, 'Coco Info Highlights History, Challenges, and Changes Necessary', https://island.lk, 8 August 2011.

21 Jerry Lorenzo, *Coconut Champion: Franklin Baker Company of the Philippines* (Makati, 2016), p. 46.

22 Brian Gray and Connie Lo, 'The Story of Sriracha Is the Story of America', www.vice.com, 9 September 2019.

3 Southeast Asia and China

1 Tien Ly, 'Traditional Cakes of Vietnam (Lunar New Year Edition)', https://guide.cmego.com, 18 January 2019.

2 'In Vietnam Coconut Worms Still Sold Openly Despite Ban', https://tuoitrenews.vn, 11 August 2016.

3 Nicholas Lander, 'Thai Cuisine in British Pubs', *Financial Times*, www.ft.com, 31 January 2009.

4 Vivienne Kruger, *Balinese Food: The Traditional Cuisine and Food Culture of Bali* (North Clarendon, VT, 2014), pp. 18–19.
5 Ibid., p. 30.
6 Adi Renaldi, 'Do We Bury Our Baby's Placenta Out of Myth or Medical Necessity?', www.vice.com, 5 October 2017.
7 Tim Cheung, 'Your Pick: World's 50 Best Foods', https://edition.cnn.com, 12 July 2017.
8 Edira Putri, 'The Philosophy of Rendang Curry', https://theculturetrip.com, 25 October 2018.
9 Kruger, *Balinese Food*, p. 26.
10 Daniel Lawrence, 'Chinese Experts Teach Coconut Carving Techniques in Seychelles', www.seychellesnewsagency.com, 30 September 2017.
11 'Folklore of Hainan-coconut', www.absolutechinatours.com, accessed 8 November 2019.
12 Li Anlan, 'Cuckoo for Coconuts! Tropical Fruit a Hainan Staple', https://archive.shine.cn, 10 June 2015.
13 'Wenchang Chicken', www.ehainan.gov.cn, accessed 7 November 2019.
14 Laurie Chen, 'Coconut Milk Gives You Bigger Breasts, Chinese Drink Ad Insists', www.scmp.com, 13 February 2019.

4 South Asia

1 'A Lovely Bunch of Coconuts', http://museumblog.winterthur.org, 25 November 2015.
2 N. M. Nayer, *The Coconut: Phylogeny, Origins, and Spread* (Cambridge, MA, 2017), p. 18.
3 L. N. Revathy, 'Marico Aims to Give Coconut Farming a Boost Through Kalpavriksha Program', www.thehindubusinessline.com, 17 September 2018.
4 'India: On the Coconut Palm', www.earthstoricz.com, accessed 10 November 2019.
5 Nayer, *The Coconut*, p. 18.

6 'Attukal Pongala', www.keralatourism.com, accessed 11 November 2019.
7 Alka Ranjan, ed., *The Illustrated Mahabharata: The Definitive Guide to India's Greatest Epic* (London, 2017), p. 83.
8 Dovita Aranha, 'Queen of Spice: The Mumbai Homemakers Keeping Bottle Masala Tradition Alive', www.thebetterindia.com, 20 May 2019.
9 A.G.S. Kariyawasan, *Buddist Ceremonies and Rituals of Sri Lanka* (Kandy, 1995), pp. 6–9.
10 'Everything You Need to Know About Sri Lankan Kiribath', www.thatswhatshehad.com, 18 July 2016.
11 Ibid.
12 'Sri Lankan Cuisine', https://lakpura.com, accessed 11 November 2019.
13 A. M. Cassim, 'Brace Yourself: Watalappam Season is Here', https://roar.media, 5 July 2016.
14 Marianne North, *Recollections of a Happy Life* (New York, 1894), p. 322.
15 *Official Guide to the North Gallery, Royal Gardens Kew* [1914], 6th edn (London, 2009), p. 35.

5 The South Pacific and the Philippines

1 R. S. Roosman, 'Coconut, Breadfruit and Taro in Pacific Oral Literature', *Journal of Polynesian Society*, XXIX/2 (June 1970), pp. 219–32.
2 Dorothee van Hoerschelmann, 'The Religious Meaning of the Samoan Kava Ceremony', *Anthropos*, CX (1995), pp. 193–5.
3 Cited in Stephen Boykewich, 'Corporate Green, Meet Coconut Theology', https://sojo.net, 11 November 2011.
4 Tori Avey, 'Paul Gauguin – His Life, His Work, His Menus', https://toriavey.com, 5 June 2015.
5 Paul Laudon, *Matisse in Tahiti* (Paris, 1999), p. 44.
6 Veronica S. Schweitzer, 'Coconut', www.coffeetimes.com, accessed 11 November 2019.

7 ‘PH Makapuno Industry Kicks off in Toronto’, www.dfa.gov.ph, 11 September 2018.

8 Josephine Cunets, ‘Food Fridays: Sweet as Coconut Pie, Philippine Style’, www.wsj.com, 25 October 2013.

6 Africa and the Middle East

1 Som Prakash Verma, *The Illustrated Baburnama* (New York, 2016), p. 351.

2 The Heritage Lab, ‘A History of Mughal Cuisine Through Cookbooks’, www.theheritagelab.in, 23 January 2017.

3 Ibid.

4 Tim Mackintosh, ed., *Travels of Ibn Battutah* (London, 2003), p. 81.

5 Adam Liaw, ‘Kuku Paka (African Chicken and Coconut Curry)’, www.goodfood.com.au, accessed 9 April 2021.

6 Sneha Datar, ‘Chaklama – Omani Baked Coconut Sweet’, www.snehasrecipe.blogspot.com, accessed 11 November 2019.

7 Salma Yassin, ‘Coconut Addicted! . . . Here’s Egyptian Sobia Drink’, www.see.news.com, 7 May 2019.

8 Ruth Oliver, ‘Stock Up on Coconut’, *Jerusalem Post*, 14 March 2013.

9 ‘Coconut and Lemons Peri-Peri Sauce’, www.nandos.com, accessed 11 November 2019.

10 ‘East African-inspired Coconut Curry Rice (Wali Wa Nazi)’, https://foodsfromafrica.com, 9 July 2016.

11 Gabeba Baderoon, *Regarding Muslims: From Slavery to Post-Apartheid* (Johannesburg, 2014), p. 93.

12 ‘Coco de Mar: A Delicious Fruit with a Suggestively Shaped Seed’, www.atlasobscura.com, accessed 21 November 2019.

13 Mike Benayoun, ‘Angola: Cocada Amarela’, www.196flavors.com, accessed 11 November 2019.

14 Michael Ashu Agbor and Sudeshni Naidoo, ‘Ethnomedicinal Plants Used by Traditional Healers

to Treat Oral Health Problems in Cameroon', *Journal of Evidence-based Complementary and Alternative Medicine*, www.pubmed.ncbi.nlm.nih.gov, 1 October 2015.

7 Europe and the Americas

1 Daniel Robinson, *Confronting Biopiracy* (New York, 2010), p. 4.
2 Ibid.
3 Mary Anne Hines et al., *The Larder Invaded: Reflections on Three Centuries of Philadelphia Food and Drink* (Philadelphia, PA, 1987), pp. 73–4.
4 Richard J. Hooker, ed., *A Colonial Plantation Cookbook: The Receipt Book of Harriott Pinckney Horry, 1770* (Columbia, SC, 1984), p. 71.
5 Founding Fathers Consortium Catalog, MRC 14855246 Record number 7601, Founding Fathers Library Consortium, Mount Vernon, Virginia.
6 Interview and correspondence with Mount Vernon librarian Mary V. Thompson, Fred W. Smith National Library for the Study of George Washington, October 2019.
7 Martha Stewart, 'Mashed Red Curry Sweet Potatoes', www.marthastewart.com, accessed 12 November 2019.
8 Marie Kimball, *Thomas Jefferson's Cookbook* (Greenville, MS, 2004), pp. 101–3.
9 Ibid.
10 Kathleen E. Kennedy, 'Why 19th Century Americans Drank from Coconut Shells', www.atlasobscura.com, 4 December 2017.
11 Charles Phoenix, 'Bambrosinana', www.splendidtable.org, accessed 12 November 2019.
12 'Laura Bush's Texas Buttermilk Coconut Pie with Whipped Cream', www.americas-table.com, 4 November 2014; Martha Mueller Neff, 'Obama Family Recipes to Meet Inauguration Day in Good Taste', www.cleveland.com, 13 January 2009.

13 Nelly Lambert, 'A Coconut Cake from Emily Dickinson: Reclusive Poet, Passionate Baker', www.npr.org, 20 October 2011.

14 'Alice B. Toklas and Her Cook Book – Part Two', www.onecrumbatatime.blogspot.com, 6 September 2011.

15 Gil Marks, 'American Cakes – Lane Cake', www.toriavey.com, 11 November 2014.

16 'Is German Chocolate Cake Really German?', www.kitchenproject.com, accessed 12 November 2019.

17 'Presidential Recipes', https://theamericanmoms.com, accessed 12 November 2019.

18 'The "Cocoanut" Ice Challenge', https://blogs.sydneylivingmuseums.com.au, 20 November 2014.

19 'Bermuda Witches', www.foodsofengland.co.uk, accessed 12 November 2019.

20 'Lamington Cake History and Recipe', https://whatscookingamerica.net, accessed 12 November 2019.

21 Isabella Beeton, *Mrs. Beeton's Household Management* (London, 1899), p. 150.

22 Alice B. Toklas, *The Alice B. Toklas Cookbook* (New York, 2010), p. 117.

23 'The Cocadas of Cartagena', https://donde.co, accessed 14 November 2019.

24 Olivia Mesquita, 'Brazilian Moist Coconut Cake', www.oliviacuisine.com, 16 April 2016.

25 Abdul Rob, 'The Origins of Slave Food: Callaloo Dumplings and Saltfish', www.blackhistorymonth.org, 20 December 2016.

26 Miss G, 'Miss G's Simple Jamaican Sweet Potato Pudding Recipe', https://jamaicans.com, accessed 14 November 2019.

27 'Jamaican Run Down', www.africanbites.com, 11 May 2015.

28 Steve Bennett, 'Saoco Recipe: A Refreshing Taste of Old Cuba Campesino Life', www.uncommoncaribbean.com, accessed 14 November 2019.

29 Magdalena Ferran, '19 Popular Puerto Rican Foods You Should Try Before You Die', www.spoonuniversity.com, accessed 14 November 2019.
30 'About the Guna Indians', https://sanblas-islands.com, accessed 14 November 2019.

8 The Future of Coconut

1 'Coconut Products Market Study', Globe Newswire, www.globesnewswite.com, 22 February 2020.
2 A. Karun et al., 'Coconut (*Cocos nucifera* L.) Pollen Cryopreservation', *Cryoletters*, XXXV/5 (September 2014), pp. 407–17.
3 C. Saensuk et al., '*De Novo* Transcriptome Assembly and Identification of the Gene Conferring a "Pandan-like" Aroma in Coconut (*Cocos nucifera* L.)', *Plant Science*, CCLII (November 2016), pp. 324–34.
4 'Government Supports Coconut Farmers', www.businessghana.com, 18 March 2018.
5 D. Rezende, et al., 'Estimated Crop Loss Due to Coconut Mite and Financial Analysis of Controlling the Pest Using the Acaricide Abamectin', *Experimental and Applied Acarology*, LXIX/3 (July 2016), pp. 297–310.
6 'Coconut Oil', The Nutrition Source, Harvard School of Public Health, www.hsph.harvard.edu, accessed 14 June 2020.
7 P.I.C. Richardson et al., 'Detection of the Adulteration of Fresh Coconut Water via NMR Spectroscopy and Chemometrics', *Analyst*, CXLIV/4 (11 February 2019), pp. 1401–8.
8 'Hamona, The Premium Coconut', https://hamonacoconut.com, accessed 21 November 2019.
9 A. Naik et al., 'Production of Coconut Protein Powder from Coconut Wet Processing Waste and Its Characterization', *Applied Biochemistry and Biotechnology*, CLXVII/5 (July 2012), pp. 1290–1302.

10 Katherine Martinko, 'Cutting Out Meat and Dairy Is the Best Thing You Can Do for the Planet', www.treehugger.com, accessed 11 November 2011.

11 Jerry Lorenzo, *Coconut Champion: Franklin Baker Company of the Philippines* (Makati, 2016), p. 235.

12 Artemas Ward, *The Encyclopedia of Food* (New York, 1923), p. 124.

Select Bibliography

Besa, Amy, and Romy Dorotan, *Memories of Philippine Kitchens: Stories and Recipes from Far and Near* (New York, 2006)

Bullis, Douglas, and Wendy Hutton, *Sri Lankan Cooking* (Hong Kong, 2009)

Cohen, Dan, *The Macaroon Bible* (New York, 2003)

Deeter, Annie, *The Coconut Bible: The Complete Coconut Reference Guide* (London, 2015)

De Havilland, Alaina, *Pacific Palate: Cuisines of the Sun* (New York, 1998)

De Neef, Janet, *Fragrant Rice: My Continuing Love Affair with Bali* (Hong Kong, 2003)

Fife, Bruce, *Cooking with Coconut Flour* (Colorado Springs, CO, 2005)

Ganeshram, Ramin, *Cooking with Coconut* (North Adams, MA, 2016)

Hafner, Dorinda, *A Taste of Africa* (Berkeley, CA, 1993)

Houston, Lynn, *Food Culture in the Caribbean* (Westport, CT, 2005)

Kannampilly, Vijayan, *The Essential Kerala Cookbook* (Haryana, 2003)

Kruger, Vivienne, *Balinese Food: The Traditional Cuisine and Food Culture of Bali* (North Clarendon, VT, 2014)

Maimal, Maya, *Savoring the Spice Coast of India: Fresh Flavors of Kerala* (New York, 2000)

Marcus, Jacqueline, *Healing Power of Coconut* (Morton Grove, IL, 2017)

Mims, Ben, *Coconuts* (New York, 2017)
Mowe, Rosalind, ed., *Culinaria Southeast Asia* (Berlin, 2008)
Nayer, N. M., *The Coconut: Phylogeny, Origins, and Spread* (Cambridge, MA, 2017)
Newport, Maria Regina Tolentino, *Coconut Kitchen: Appetizers and Main Dishes* (Mandaluyong, 2017)
Sivanathan, Prakash K., and Niranjala M. Ellawala, *Sri Lanka: The Cookbook* (London, 2017)
Wilson, Laura Agar, *Coconut Oil* (Brighton, 2017)

Websites and Associations

Websites

'Is Coconut a Fruit, Nut or Seed?', U.S. Library of Congress
www.loc.gov

Coconut Timeline (Coconut Knowledge Network)
http://cocos.arecaceae.com

Food Timeline: Coconuts
www.foodtimeline.org

Deep History of Coconuts Decoded
https://source.wustl.edu

Traditional Pacific Island Crops
https://guides.library.manoa.hawaii.edu

Associations

Coconut Development Board
www.coconutboard.gov.in

International Coconut Community (ICC)
https://coconutcommunity.org

Cooking Schools

The following organizations offer cooking classes and market tours customized to include coconut.

With Locals – Indonesia, India, Sri Lanka, Thailand
www.withlocals.com

Backstreet Academy – Cambodia, Laos, Indonesia, Vietnam
www.backstreetacademy.com

Paon Bali Cooking Class – Ubud, Bali
www.paon-bali.com

Casa Luna Cooking School – Ubud, Bali
www.casalunabali.com

Viator – Luang Prabang, Laos
www.viator.com

Festivals

San Pablo Coco Festival, Philippines
www.philippines.travel.com

Narali Poornima Coconut Festival, Mumbai India
www.tourmyindia.com

Hawaii Coconut Festival
www.gohawaii.com

International Coconut Festival in Ghana
http://ghanacoconutfestival.com

Acknowledgements

We are grateful to our many friends throughout the world who generously shared their knowledge and enthusiasm for our pursuit of coconut.

Many teacher-chefs at cooking schools contributed valuable practical experience in preparing coconut dishes, including Puspa of Paon and Janet De Neefe of Casa Luna in Bali, Indonesia, and Duneeshya Bagoda in Colombo, Sri Lanka. Friends Shadow Paul, Margaret Lonzetta and Marie Coreces provided first-hand information and photographs of coconut products. Joanne Bening provided helpful advice that greatly improved our photographic illustrations. We had the pleasure of participating in a Vietnamese wedding celebration, which included preparations of coconut sweets with Loan Nguyen Kachuba and her family. We value the research of Kathleen E. Kennedy on the historical context of coconut.

A special thanks to Ulysess Guese who hosted us in his hometown of San Pablo, Philippines, during the city's annual coconut festival and made certain we visited many coconut related sites. Julian Baricuatro, organizer of the Toronto Coconut Festival, was helpful in connecting us to Amado Orden, professor at the University of Baguio, Philippines. Chef Cris Agas, of the Bay Leaf Restaurant in Baguio, created a most memorable all-coconut meal especially for us. Peter Kaman, Product Marketing Director in the U.S. office of Franklin Baker Inc., kindly introduced us to Franklin Baker Philippines, where we were welcomed by Cel Yap at the company's facilities in San Pablo.

Airbnb hosts from the Philippines to Sri Lanka were generous with their time and knowledge of coconut in their countries. We thank Elizabeth and Joseph at Aroma Homestay in Fort Kochi, Kerala, India, for fabulous coconut-focused meals, Vagira at Tree Breeze Inn in Kandy, Sri Lanka, for sharing her own wedding photos, and the whole family at Alleppey Backwater Homestay in Kerala, India, for a memorable Sadya feast. Our host at Villa Sanasuma, Sunil Assalaarach, in Bentota, Sri Lanka, treated us to delicious coconut breakfasts and snacks.

Jose and Marissa, proprietors of Connecticut Coconut Company in Shelton, Connecticut, shared a wealth of information with us about coconut sugar and coconut flour. Many thanks to the staff and participants at Education Matters, Community Matters in Cincinnati, Ohio, for their demonstration of West African recipes using coconuts. Dr Kathryn Lorenz of Lorenz Language Consultants was an early reader of the book and gave us editing and proofreading assistance, as did the Friends and Books book club in Cincinnati. We wish to thank the wonderful staff at the St Bernard Branch of the Cincinnati and Hamilton County Public Library and the staff at the library of Pennsylvania State University, Brandywine Campus, for their resources and recommendations. And last but not least, we thank our families, especially our husbands, Tom and John, who bravely sampled our coconut dishes.

Photo Acknowledgements

The authors and publishers wish to express their thanks to the below sources of illustrative material and/or permission to reproduce it.

Franklin Baker, *Coconut Champion*: p. 42; Boston Public Library: p. 106; Getty Images: pp. 8 (Saul Loeb), 37 (DeAgostini); Constance L. Kirker: pp. 6, 10, 20, 23, 24, 25, 27, 28, 29, 32, 44, 46, 51, 52, 54, 56, 57, 58, 61, 62, 70, 72, 73, 75, 77, 78, 79, 80, 89, 92, 94, 100, 101, 103, 111, 114, 116, 117, 118, 119 top and bottom, 124, 125, 131, 132, 134, 135; *Köhlers Medizinal-Pflanzen*: p. 17; Los Angeles Museum of Art: p. 122 (© Banco de México Diego Rivera Frida Kahlo Museums Trust, Mexico, DF/DACS 2021); Metropolitan Museum of Art, New York: p. 38 (Gift of J. Pierpont Morgan, 1917); Musée d'Orsay, Paris: p. 85; Museum of the Americas, Madrid: p. 41; Mary Newman: pp. 48, 90, 99; Marianne North Collection, Kew Gardens: p. 81; Pennsylvania Academy of Fine Art, Philadelphia: p. 108; Shadow Paul: pp. 86, 87; Smithsonian Institution: p. 97 (Freer Collection); Unsplash: p. 6 (Farhan Azam); Courtesy of Damayanthi Werapitiya: p. 79; Wikimedia Commons: Niklas Jonsson, the copyright holder of the image on p. 18, has published it online under conditions imposed by a Creative Commons Attribution-Share Alike 3.0 Unported License; Winterthur Museum Collection: p. 66.

Index

italic numbers refer to illustrations; **bold** to recipes